Helmuth Stoecker

Socialism with Deficits

Anpassung – Selbstbehauptung – Widerstand

Band 14

LIT

Helmuth Stoecker

SOCIALISM WITH DEFICITS

An academic life in the German Democratic Republic

Edited from the private papers by Holger Stoecker

LIT

The cover photograph, which shows the author in 1984, was taken by Andreas Trogisch, who also took the photograph on page 97. All other photographs are from the private papers of the author.

Die Deutsche Bibliothek – CIP-Einheitsaufnahme

Stoecker, Helmuth
Socialism with Deficits : An academic life in the German Democratic Republic / Helmuth Stoecker. – Hamburg : LIT, 2000
    (Anpassung - Selbstbehauptung - Widerstand ; 14.)
    ISBN 3-8258-3990-7

NE: GT

© LIT VERLAG Münster – Hamburg – London
    Grindelberg 15a 20144 Hamburg Tel. 040–44 64 46 Fax 040–44 14 22

Distributed in North America by:

Transaction Publishers
New Brunswick (U.S.A.) and London (U.K.)

Transaction Publishers
Rutgers University
35 Berrue Circle
Piscataway, NJ 08854

Tel.: (732) 445 – 2280
Fax: (732) 445 – 3138
for orders (U.S. only):
toll free 888-999-6778

Contents

Editorial note

The following memoir was written between 1991 and 1994, prompted by the wide public interest in the extinct GDR. Helmuth Stoecker wrote this text, which was not intended to be a complete autobiography, primarily for an English-speaking audience. He therefore wrote it in English, to which he had felt a particularly close attachment since the years spent in emigration in Great Britain during his youth. The author worked on this memoir until shortly before his death. Although work on it was well advanced, it was not possible for him to complete the finishing touches. He was therefore unable to integrate the advice and suggestions of friends, colleagues and family members.

The text is published according to the manuscript in the personal papers, with some minor shortening of unfinished parts. The only things which I add are the photos. I was encouraged to publish this memoir, despite its partially fragmentary nature, by young academics from English-speaking countries. Their interest lay less in individual facts and events from the history of the GDR, but more in how these were witnessed by somebody who had lived through the GDR and had, in his subject area, done his bit to shape it. Helmuth Stoecker's multifaceted relationship to the GDR is knowledgeably described in the foreword by Irina Filatova, who was closely associated with the author over many years, both as colleague and friend. I am most grateful for her understanding words.

I would also like to thank everybody who contributed to this publication for their help and support. Particular thanks go to Josie McLellan for her careful editing of the text.

Holger Stoecker

The World That Was Ours

I shall not write Helmuth Stoecker's biography. Nor shall I attempt an analysis of his research and writing. I am not qualified to do this in the first place for Helmuth mostly wrote in German and I do not read or speak this language. But I also think that it would be unfair for me to do this for two reasons: I am a foreigner who may understand how the socialist world functioned while it lasted but who was never directly involved in academic or political debate in the GDR; and I was a friend of Helmuth's which may add understanding but is not conducive to objectivity.

What I shall try to do is to explain how I understand Helmuth's views and political perceptions, not as a prominent German historian and a well-known specialist in African history, but as a human being, an intellectual within the tough ideological world of socialist academia.

When was it that I first met Helmuth? It must have been about 1976, because by 1978, when he invited me to visit the GDR, we had already been good friends, if mainly by correspondence.

Our acquaintance began with me taking him, a senior colleague and Africanist historian, around Moscow. At that time I did not know his work at all, for no Russian or English translations of his books on Africa had been published yet. Helmuth was a guest of the Soviet Academy of Sciences, or, to be more exact, of the Department of African History of the Institute of General History, with which he was to develop a permanent and friendly link. The Academy of Sciences did not have a complement of professional interpreters on its staff, at least not for guests at the level of ordinary professors from socialist countries. The inviting departments had to look after their guests themselves – and this is what I was asked to help with.

For us Soviet academics, a visit of a foreign colleague was always an event, even though the majority of such visits were paid by colleagues from our side of the Berlin Wall. This visit proved to be particularly useful for me. I have always been interested in the history of colonialism and its effects on African societies, and Helmuth specialised in German colonial policy and knew British colonial policy very well indeed. During our slow walks along the Moskva-river or less pleasurable long rides in the crowded Moscow underground we discussed specific features of colonialism in Kenya, Namibia, Zimbabwe and the Portuguese colonies and argued about the nature of society and the liberation struggle in South Africa and about the future of all these countries.

Helmuth's knowledge of his discipline and of the literature on his subject was profound and detailed, and I benefited from this tremendously. Whatever topic sprang up in our conversations he was scrupulously exact and correct to the smallest detail about his sources and wording. We discussed research, academic plans, recent publications, students and curricula. We shared a joke and, of course, a good old gossip about our colleagues – Africanists from our own and other socialist countries – added spice to our conversation.

There was, however, much more to our friendship than purely professional interest. Helmuth was deeply attracted by Russian and Soviet history but knew little of Soviet realities. He was interested in day-to-day life, culture, people's perceptions and micro-politics, and during his many visits to Moscow my colleagues and I tried to show him a representative selection of these.

He, for his part, invited me (as well as some of my colleagues) to visit him and his family in Berlin. It was thanks to this invitation that I was abroad for the first time in my life and I shall never forget this experience. Nor shall I ever forget Helmuth's warm and understanding generosity. To give just one example: Helmuth invited me to accompany him on a wonderful trip to Thuringia which I would not have been able to afford on my own. It was an incredible stroke of luck, a breakthrough for me, as it would have been for the overwhelming majority of Soviet citizens who were locked up within the Soviet borders. In other words, we had a lot to offer one another .

But Helmuth struck me at once as a true believer. Not only did he believe in socialist ideals but also in socialist rhetoric. He sincerely believed in the just cause of world socialism, in the virtues of the Soviet Union and in the overwhelming importance of the interests of the "socialist camp". He was sincere, honest and serious about all these things which few of us academics of the post-war Soviet generations could take seriously. For him there may have been mistakes, misjudgement and misdeeds on the part of the leadership but all these had nothing to do with the true socialist cause and could have been avoided.

The GDR was his true passion. I am not sure that there were many things in Helmuth's life that were more important to him than the existence and the righteousness of his country. I sometimes had a feeling that he was engaged in a never-ending argument with an imaginary opponent of socialist Germany as if it always needed protection. Not from me, of course: I would have never dared to upset him with anything more than questions. Maybe his imaginary opponent was West

German news programmes which Helmuth habitually denounced as a pack of lies and cheap propaganda but which he nevertheless watched alongside with the rest of the East German population. Or it could have been Western media as a whole. It could even have been a collective image of some of his less convinced neighbours or colleagues. Whoever it was, the essence of Helmuth's message to this opponent was, once and for all, that the system was infallible, it was only concrete leaders who could sometimes go wrong.

Normally I kept away from people with such unbending faith because I suspected them of being either dishonest or politically naive. But Helmuth was a politically sophisticated academic with wide horizons and an expert in international relations. And he was a good Marxist. Not only could he quote the works of Marx and Engels on every subject of interest to him, he understood the spirit of Marxist philosophy and was very strict about Marxist dialectics. But he believed in the overwhelming significance and universal applicability of this theory. I still remember his awe-stricken expression when he whispered to me at a conference: "But she is not exactly a Marxist!" as we listened to a Czech colleague's presentation on (if I remember the topic correctly) traditional beliefs in pre-colonial Uganda.

Gradually I developed a feeling that Helmuth was lonely – politically lonely which for him meant generally lonely for he was a political animal. In his memoirs he mentions only his unhappiness with his colleagues, Africanist historians in Leipzig, who were less professional than he but got more acclaim. In Helmuth's view this was because they were at Leipzig University which was officially proclaimed the centre of the GDR's African studies, and he was in Berlin, the only Africanist historian among linguists and specialists on Asia. But he did not seem to be particularly close to his colleagues in Berlin either. I think that the problem was deeper than the unfortunate decision of the GDR's leadership to concentrate African studies in Leipzig. Helmuth was politically lonely, maybe without even realising it himself. For some of those who got to know him he must have been too ardent a supporter of the regime; for others he was too much of a non-conformist. Both were true – and this was Helmuth's biggest problem.

Was it by chance that he did not achieve more career-wise? Of course, he was a tenured professor at East Germany's best university but he had many qualities which could have taken him much higher, in fact, to the highest positions within the Party or state institutions or at least in the Academy of Sciences. This did not happen – and not by sheer bad luck. Helmuth was an intellectual – a category which communists, starting with Lenin, seldom trusted. And he spent his youth and was educated in Britain – a serious blot on a biography of a proper communist. Had Helmuth been a Soviet communist, such baggage would, most probably, have affected his fate in a much more dramatic and radical way, particularly in the late 1930s. The German socialist state was, by necessity, more lenient towards such cases but it did not help any career. I think, however, that Helmuth's views would have been an obstacle to his career in any case.

The Leipzig school of African studies was the most dogmatic in the whole "socialist camp" (which, of course, does not mean to say that all academics there were dogmatic) and this was what the authorities felt most comfortable with – much more than with Helmuth's intellectualism, professionalism and deep understanding of Marxist theory. Helmuth belonged neither among unquestioning believers, nor among cynical careerists who did not have any beliefs at all. It was these two categories that had the best career opportunities in our socialist world. Helmuth was a rational believer, he had to consider a political measure and then to accept or reject it, and this was not what the GDR authorities wanted from their citizens – or Soviet authorities from theirs.

Helmuth's position was closest to that of the old guard of communists – those who were there before the war. These were the people among whom Helmuth grew up and among whom he had friends. It was these people who believed in socialism as a principle and in the overwhelming value of its practical embodiment, the socialist state, but who felt that they had every right to discuss, criticise (within the Party circles only, of course), and accept or reject the actions of their leaders. It is not by accident that Helmuth often quotes his mother, one of the old guard, as the greatest authority on Party matters. For the GDR government they were an uncomfortable lot. They could not be controlled and they had to be respected. They would be glorified posthumously but those who were alive were unpredictable and therefore dangerous.

The position of such people was not without contradiction. They wanted a better socialism, open, democratic, humane and just, but they wanted to achieve this ideal through Party domination, in fact control over the whole of society. They felt that they knew the ultimate truth and that they were the movers of processes of global importance. They bore an air of great superiority, almost of arrogance, towards outsiders – and at the same time a feeling of great humility, almost submissiveness towards the Party. This explains at least some of the glaring contradictions in Helmuth's perceptions as he presents them in his memoirs.

Helmuth clearly indicates that he blames failures of the regime on the Party leadership. At the same time he mentions his belief that this very leadership was better informed than he was when he did not agree with them or could find no logical explanation for their actions. Historians have yet to explain what it was in the social and political climate of the day that produced this passionate faith in the middle of the most rational of centuries. Faith does not require any logic – and here is Helmuth passionately denouncing the leadership for not trusting the youth enough to allow them to travel on the one hand, and for allowing the majority of East German citizens to watch West German TV on the other. Helmuth believes that Soviet socialism was, generally, more developed and superior to that of his country but when he describes the worst sides of Soviet influence on the GDR he seems to think that they were good enough for Russia but not for Germany.

Despite the seemingly dispassionate style Helmuth's memoirs are a passionate text – but he reserves his passion for politics, not for personal life. It is an autobiography – but not really Helmuth's personally. It is rather an autobiography of a collective citizen of his country, devoted and politically conscious. There is little room for personal emotions in it. Helmuth's private life and family are there only to introduce the author and to present certain sides of social welfare in the GDR. It is a pity. The attractions of the GDR would be much more obvious to the reader had he been given a chance to see not only society as a whole but also a deeper look at people's everyday life, the aspirations, achievements and disappointments. These were the attractions I saw in the 1970s and 1980s.

Through this personal perspective the GDR looked unbelievably wealthier, cleaner, better fed, better dressed and better organised than the USSR. Quiet music playing during meals at Helmuth's spacious flat, his huge comfortable study, measured steady pace of life, the shining kitchen, spotless staircase, clean streets, shops full of goods, food and comfortable clothes, wonderfully tasty sausages and beer at every corner (Helmuth disapproved of my passion for them but Erika, who knew Soviet life much better, understood), virtually no queues.

And a wonderful feeling of freedom. What a luxury – they could buy foreign newspapers, they could watch West German TV, they could read émigré and other banned (banned in the USSR that is) literature in the State and University libraries, they could travel abroad and Africanists could even go to Africa. Helmuth writes that during the

1970s academic travel became more difficult for the GDR Africanists and historians – but they could still do it! At that time most of us, Soviet Africanists, could not even dream of such luck as attendance at international conferences, visits to Africa and particularly opportunities to work there or in West European and American libraries and archives. All this was not easily accessible to East German Africanists either – but it was still possible. Looking at the GDR through Soviet eyes one could almost believe in the bright future of socialism, at least in that country.

But there were other images of the GDR that are firmly stuck in my memory from my first visits there. I remember a small town in Thuringia with a Soviet military base or a military object right next to a beautiful medieval cathedral. An ugly high fence topped with barbed wire completely spoilt the central square. The locals behaved as if they failed to notice it, they looked past it as if it was not there. Here and there Soviet soldiers, small and thin among tall German youth, with non-smiling expressionless faces, obviously on a day's furlough, walked slowly in tense pairs through the laughing and chatting Saturday spring crowd. Nobody spoke to them, people looked through them as they would through an empty space but made way to let them pass, carefully avoiding accidentally touching them.

I told Helmuth how dreadful I felt about the feelings of both sides and how tactless it was on the part of the Soviet military to put their base right in the middle of the town. He answered that it may have been not the best place but that the general attitude to Soviet troops was good, and it was only the language problem that prevented closer communication. "The same soldiers would be warmly welcomed if they visited a factory or a school with an interpreter", he said. "And hated quietly even more", I thought. I felt absolutely sure that this situation could not last.

On another occasion the son of another German friend showed me the Berlin wall at a close range. He knew a block of flats in a side street in Berlin, which almost overhung the wall. The window on the third or fourth floor was wide open, although it was winter, and the window-sill polished to a shine by visitors' coats. The place was obviously well attended. I looked out and discovered that the wall was not actually one wall, but two, one next to the other, separated by a carefully raked strip of sand a couple of metres wide. It was heavily guarded on our side, and on the other side there was an elevated platform so that the curious public could have a look at the socialist part of their city. The platform was rather close and we could see the faces of a couple who happened to be there at that moment. They looked at us, and we looked at them. None of us smiled or laughed or shouted anything, or waved a hand. We just stood there looking at one another for quite a while. And then they started to get down and I said that I want to get home, to the Stoeckers, right away because I was freezing.

In fact I was on the brink of crying. In the evening I told Helmuth that I did not believe that cutting a living body of one nation into two was at all viable and that people will not take it. I think that it was the only time that I was so cruel. But Helmuth was not offended. He patiently explained to me that East Germans had become a separate nation: they had a different economy, a different territory, a different culture, a different lifestyle, a perception of themselves as a different nation and even a different language because their reality was different, and it was reality that created a language. He also told me that if the GDR were to disappear this would lead to an upsurge of nationalism and possibly even fascism. I thought that it was all dogmatic and formalistic nonsense. What Helmuth gave me here was Stalin's list of characteristics of the nation which were in my view inapplicable to the GDR.

I thought of Helmuth when the Berlin wall went down. I thought that he must have been devastated and frustrated not only because of the collapse of the GDR, but also because his approach to the history of his country had been proved wrong. Now, a decade later, when I read about frustrations of former East Germans in their new motherland and about the upsurge of nationalism in the former East Germany, I often think of Helmuth again. I still think that I was right and he was wrong but maybe he was less wrong than I realised at the time.

When I meet friends from the former socialist countries we often reflect on how little we had realised how different our socialist world was to the other one in which we suddenly found ourselves, and how long it would take us to overcome the difference, if ever. We have a common past, whether good or bad, a common legacy and many common problems which the rest of the world just does not understand or in which it is not interested. Helmuth's memoirs are a glimpse into that past, into the world that was ours.

Irina Filatova (Durban, South Africa)

Then let us pray that come it may
(As come it will for a' that)
That sense and worth, o'er a' the earth,
Shall bear the gree, and a' that.
For a' that, and a' that,
It's coming yet for a' that,
That man to man the warld o'er
Shall brothers be for a' that.

Robert Burns

Prefatory note

This little book is an attempt to help readers in English-speaking countries to understand more fully why the German Democratic Republic (GDR), outside its borders the object of emotions ranging from point-blank rejection to uncritical enthusiasm, was created, how it developed (with an emphasis on university life and historical science), and why it could disappear from the map. Its collapse was a momentous event which has been interpreted in many ways. Perhaps the experience, observations, and reflections of an intellectual who lived and worked in this republic from its founding to its demise can throw light on some parts of its many-sided and complicated history. What they obviously cannot claim to provide is any definitive explanations.
Although I am a historian by profession the book is not a work of scholarship but rather has the character of memoirs interspersed with passages on the development of the GDR. As not only historians know, memoirs are often tendentious and factually unreliable. I hope that my point of view has not impaired my sense of realities, and I have tried to avoid factual inaccuracies by checking up the facts mentioned whenever possible. I am especially indebted to those of my friends and former colleagues who patiently answered my questions.

Helmuth Stoecker

Return to Berlin.
As the inter-Allied train from Paris approached Berlin, I stood in the corridor and looked out on a landscape which had become quite unfamiliar to me. The English telephone engineer in our compartment joined me, looked out for a moment and asked me "How long ago did you leave Berlin?" When I answered "Fourteen years ago", he exclaimed "Oh my God!" and gave me a compassionate look.

Coming from London, my mother, my sister and I had joined the train at Ostend the day before. Although it was reserved for Allied personnel, we were given a friendly reception by the other travellers in an only half full compartment after we had explained that we were German refugees from Nazism returning home. They were the English engineer from British headquarters in Berlin, a female interpreter in U.S. uniform evidently of German-Jewish origin, and a French sergeant who, knowing no English, confined himself to amiable gestures. In the company of these representatives of the Western powers, our journey had been quite agreeable. On arrival we were greeted warmly by old friends of my mother, with whom she had lived for several years and taken part in resistance activities before leaving for England in 1938.

After bringing her children to England in 1933 she had returned to Berlin in order to do what she could for my father, who had been arrested soon after Hitler's appointment as Chancellor and then, in the course of six terrible years, gone through three concentrationcamps. Much weakened and without medical aid, he died in a typhoid epidemic in Buchenwald concentrationcamp six months before war began. My mother had left Germany only after she had lost all hope of obtaining his release and could no longer visit him or send him anything.

Our parents had decided to send us to England because our family had some English connections: my mother's father was an Englishman who had settled in the Rhineland when still young, and my father's elder sister had married an Englishman. But these family links had virtually lapsed and turned out to be of no help. Therefore British refugee aid committees had taken charge of us and seen to it that my sister and I were sent to English schools.

At first we were sent to A.S. Neill's famous Summerhill School in Leiston, Suffolk. Neill had been kind enough to accept us without fees, but I suppose I was not enough of a problem child to fit in there. After a year the Sheffield Refugee Committee undertook to look after me and placed me, with the assistance of the Quaker headmaster, at King Edward VII School, the best school in that city and one of the three best grammar schools in the north of England. There I stayed for five years, obtaining a better education than the great majority of English youngsters could hope for at that time.

During term I had lived with a childless middle class couple – Captain Stuart Lamont was managing director of a coal trading firm – and had come to know their world intimately. But after a phase of adaptation was over, I realised that it would never be my world, although the Lamonts were always good to me and, as a reasonably good pupil, I was fully accepted at the school.

Decisive for my future were people of a very different kind. During the five years at King Edward's I spent all school holidays without exception from the first day to the last in London or, in summer, somewhere in the countryside with Ivor Montagu and his wife, known to friends as "Hell".

After arriving in Berlin we stayed with our friends who lived in the eastern part of the city for the first three weeks and then moved to a small flat. We bought most of the furniture needed from the local authorities who had confiscated all goods abandoned by Nazis who had fled to the Western zones of occupation or simply disappeared.

My English travelling companion's compassion was understandable: The four sectors of Berlin in April 1947 presented the picture of a city in ruins. Especially the centre, but also most of the suburbs were hardly more than heaps of rubble which made many streets impassable for vehicles and often dangerous for pedestrians. Where houses were still standing and inhabited, window panes had frequently been replaced by cardboard; in many houses staircases were risky to use because, damaged by bombs or shells, they could collapse at any time. Houses with undamaged roofs were rare. The few trams and local trains were incredibly crammed with poorly clad, evil smelling people – there was almost no soap. Food rations, though higher in Berlin than in other towns of the Soviet Zone of Occupation were too small to subsist on, and so tens of thousands of city dwellers habitually travelled to the countryside on dangerously overcrowded trains in order to obtain food in exchange for some possession or other – money was not accepted by the farmers and small peasants. At the same time countless works of art and antique furniture plundered from the homes of dispossessed estate owners who had usually "gone West" took the same route in exchange for American cigarettes, shoes, clothing, soap, razor blades etc.

The black market flourished as the shortage of food, clothing, coal and other everyday necessities was far worse than in Britain during the war. The population in general had not yet recovered from the catastrophe of 1945 and from the extremely hard winter of 1946-7.

The collapse of 1945 had not only been political and material but also moral: there was widespread apathy and despondency, and not a little downright demoralisation. People were not "nice to each other". The presence of four military administrations in the city led to much uncertainty and nervousness about the future. Young people I visited in the American sector who had hoped that a united Left would lead to a brighter future were disillusioned and had decided to emigrate as soon as possible.

During my first weeks in Berlin I tried as best as I could to inform myself about the situation. I roamed about at random and was again and again appalled at the scenes of misery and destruction. At the same time I could not help noticing traces of the evil past, such as the many precious fur coats worn by women which had obviously been plundered by German soldiers in the Soviet Union. One day I climbed about alone in the deserted ruins of Hitler's New Chancellery, studying the inhuman and barbaric Nordic warriors depicted in the reliefs to be found on many walls.

The newspapers, strictly controlled by the administration of the sector they were printed in, were not very informative. Here, and later in the Soviet Zone, I found that many people bought them only because of the local notifications on rations or other matters of everyday life they published, or as a substitute for toilet paper, which was unobtainable. Therefore I spoke not only with the old friends we were staying with but also with a number of friends and acquaintances we knew well from years spent together in exile and with everyone else prepared to answer my questions.

I was told that the economic situation was much aggravated by the enormous losses of manpower during the war and in the Soviet Zone by reparations to the Soviet Union and Poland. The systematic destruction of Soviet railway lines by the retreating German armies, for example, led to the dismantling of many railway lines needed for the reconstruction of the devastated areas of Byelorussia. As a result a great number of lines, including such an important one as the Berlin-Leipzig line, were reduced to a single track until the early 1950s.

Prisoners of war were returning from French, Belgian and British camps, and from the United States, but as yet only in very small numbers from the Soviet Union and Poland, where most of them had to work on reconstruction sites for years to come. In view of the truly terrible losses people in the East had to suffer as the result of Nazi aggression this was understandable, hard as it was for these prisoners and their families. But the delay in releasing them hardly contributed to making the Soviet Union more popular in Germany, where the attitude to it was often one of ill-concealed fear or contempt. Only a small minority would concede in 1947 that "the Russian" was anything but a barbarian. The behaviour of some Soviet units on entering Germany in 1945 had, in the opinion of many, confirmed Goebbel's propaganda against the Soviet Union. It was not realised or not admitted that pilfering and worse by Soviet troops in the first weeks after the end of hostilities were the result of the terrible crimes of Hitler's armies and occupation authorities in the Soviet Union in the years before, and also, to some degree, of the savagery engendered by all wars.

There had been no large-scale warfare on German territory (except for East Prussia) since 1866 and no plundering by foreign troops since the times of Napoleon.

There was no sign whatever of any Nazi activity. In the Soviet Zone and East Berlin the "de-nazification" demanded by the Potsdam Agreement was much facilitated by the general exodus of former Nazi party officials, leaders of the Hitler Youth, state bureaucrats and almost all other seized by panicky fear of "the Russians". These people had nearly all gone off to the American or British Zones of Occupation where they expected – as it turned out correctly – to be much less endangered. The great numbers of former nominal members of the Nazi party were politically passive. Some tried to make good by working very hard.

Working hard, often under extremely difficult conditions, were great parts of the undernourished, badly clothed and badly housed working class, among whom the Socialist Unity Party (SED) was beginning to gain some influence. But the daily struggle for a minimal existence left little time for a seeming luxury such as politics. The party had come into being in 1946 by the merger of the Communist and Social Democratic parties (KPD and SPD), both re-established soon after the destruction of the Nazi regime. All positions in the united party were until 1949 held by two persons with equal rights, one a former communist, the other a former social democrat. A few weeks after arriving in Berlin my mother and I joined the SED, to which nearly all our friends belonged. At this time anyone could become a party member, except for former Nazis, former army officers, former members of the upper class and persons with a criminal record. Quite a few people had joined because they expected that membership would bring them some advantage. With my party card, I was given a ticket for a meeting to celebrate the first anniversary of the unification in the centre of Berlin.

It was attended by many old members. A number of well-known party leaders spoke, among others the veteran social democrat Eugen Ernst who had been police president of Berlin in 1919/20 and had played an important part in defeating the left wing rising of January 1919 in Berlin. Another old social democrat, the president of the Trade Union Federation (ADGB) before Hitler's assumption of power, Theodor Leipart, had sent the meeting a message of support just before his death a few weeks before. It was read out to the standing audience. The speakers praised working class unity from various points of view.

During the meeting I watched the audience closely to see if there were any signs of animosity between people taking part. Communists and social democrats had been such bitter enemies in the past that such signs were conceivable, but there were none. The meeting confirmed the impression I had gained from reports received in London: there might well have been some pressure on social democrats by Soviet administrations on the local level to unite with the communists, but such pressure was largely unnecessary.

The truth was that the social democrats were divided as they had been ever since 1933. Some of their leaders in the British and American Zones, such as Hans Vogel, Erich Ollenhauer and Kurt Schumacher, were strictly against cooperation with the communists, let alone unification, others wavered, and leaders in the Soviet Zone, such as Theodor Leipart, Georg Gradnauer, Otto Grotewohl, Otto Buchwitz and Friedrich Ebert junior, wanted a "Party of Socialist Unity".

The closest friend of my father in his youth, Michael Schröder, whose acquaintance I made a year later, had been chairman of the SPD in Cologne and member of the Prussian parliament during the Weimar Republic. As leader of the social democrats in Wittenberg after 1945 he was active in bringing about unification in the whole of Sachsen-Anhalt, and told me in 1960 that he was happy to have had the chance of playing a part in re-uniting the socialist movement.

But there was opposition in the Soviet Zone, too, especially in Leipzig and Dresden, which had been strongholds of the SPD up to 1933. Such a fundamental matter needed to be explained and discussed by party members, and the decision to unify earlier than originally intended hadn't left sufficient time for discussion. Therefore social democrats in some places felt that the decision had been taken without their express consent. Most of the opponents and doubters joined the new party nonetheless and adapted to it in the following years.

In the autumn of 1947 – to anticipate a little – the secretary of the party organisation at a railway repair base in Leipzig invited me to speak to his comrades at one of their monthly after-work meetings. On entering the hall in which the meeting took place, I found about 30 members sitting in the front rows. Another 30 or so were sitting at some distance toward the back. The secretary told me that the former communists were sitting at the front, and the former social democrats at the back. Obviously the merger had not been consummated here and therefore I explained at some length that only the split in the working class movement since the first world war had made possible the Hitler regime and the catastrophe of 1945. After I had finished some of the former communists supported me while the former social democrats kept silent.

For years to come it was always easy to recognise which party a speaker at such meetings came from: social democrats in free speech appealed to the feelings of their audience, referring only to facts know to all. The communists appealed to their reason, arguing with facts not everyone knew (even with statistics). The communists were usually not impressive as orators. My audience at that meeting had obviously not been swept from their feet by a university student accustomed to elaborate argument, sound as the reasoning may have been.

The two parties had been too different from each other for the merger to be a simple matter. Not only their aims, but also the composition of their membership, the demands made on members, the organisational structure, the methods of campaigning and the attitude to Marxist theory had developed along diverse lines. The degree of difference might well be compared to that between Roman Catholics and Protestants.

The social democrats who rejected the SED either moved to the West or retreated into inactivity. In the fifties I made the acquaintance of such a social democrat, a retired printer living in the centre of Leipzig, who had been a devoted trade unionist all his life. On the wall of the room he rented me for a few weeks there was a large old portrait of August Bebel. A kindly old man, he lived on his memories and appeared to take little notice of his surroundings.

The merger of the two parties had effected further development in the Soviet Zone. It had given people the driving force needed for gradual advance out of the deep chasm into which the Hitler regime had driven them. Symbolic for the newly found unity of democrats and socialists will always be for me not the well-known picture taken in 1946 of two marching columns converging towards each other against a background of ruins but a demonstration which took place two years later to commemorate the centenary of the uprising of the "lower orders" of Berlin in March 1848. Cold rain poured unceasingly on the long columns of undernourished and poorly clad factory workers, railwaymen, builders and others, who had followed the call of the party in their thousands to file past the graves of those who had given their lives one hundred years before. Having no umbrellas most of them were drenched to the skin, but they ignored the appeals of a number of British and American officers to go home and stamped doggedly on. It was a scene I shall never forget. In the gap between two columns an elderly gentleman wearing spats marched alone. It was Dr. Alfred Meusel, professor of modern history at the Humboldt University.

As a student in Leipzig.
On one of the last days of April I went off to Leipzig to enrol as a student at the university there. My mother and sister stayed in Berlin in our flat, which remained my home address and to which I frequently returned. There was no need to support them: as a victim of Nazi persecution and an invalid, my mother was soon granted a small pension, enough to live on modestly, and my sister was given a scholarship at an art school. My mother's health, undermined by years of pulmonary tuberculosis, had been seriously weakened by all she had gone through. During the V-2 attacks on London she had collapsed completely, and after she had spent four weeks in hospital I had to take her to Oxford, where she was safe from air-raids and remained till the end of the war. For the rest of her life – she was then forty-eight – she was unable to work.

My choice had been between Leipzig and Berlin. At Berlin I could have joined a group of young people with an anti-Nazi background who were studying history under the guidance of Meusel, the excellent Marxist historian mentioned above. But when an old friend of my mother's told me that a faculty for social sciences was to be founded at Leipzig University as a counter-weight to the distinctly conservative faculties of art and economics, the idea of studying at such an institution fascinated me. It would, I thought, give me a better chance than Berlin of helping to transform university life in a democratic and progressive direction, even if only as a student. After thinking it over, I decided on Leipzig.

The decision turned out to be a fortunate one, although my first experiences in this old centre of German culture, where Goethe had studied and the German (National) Library was situated, were hardly encouraging. After taking a furnished room in the centre of the city I discovered that my landlady was the wife of a former Nazi party official interned in the American Zone. When I indignantly moved out she implored me to give her American cigarettes. On the same evening I went to a restaurant nearby with the intention of having supper. When I asked the waiter what they had to offer he and other guests looked at me as though I had come from the moon: the restaurant had nothing to offer except some cheap lemonade and bad beer.

The new faculty, known as the Gewifa (faculty of social science), had had a difficult birth. The Rector, Vice Chancellor Professor Gadamer, and the Senate were unable to prevent its foundation, but they did what they could to delay it and to hinder the appointment of Marxists as university teachers. In spite of the resistance of prominent members of the Senate such as the philosophers Litt and Gadamer and the jurist de Boor, who attempted to have expelled Nazi professors re-appointed, the Gewifa succeeded in winning a number of excellent men as teachers.

The first was Professor Arthur Baumgarten, a noted and venerable Swiss sociologist and philosopher. The chair of economics was entrusted to Friedrich Behrens, a Marxist who had been a member of the Socialist Workers' Party (SAP). He was the first dean of the faculty. His lectures on the history of political economy (including a thorough treatment of Marx' "Kapital") soon gained him much popularity among the students. The physicist Gerhard Harig, until 1945 a prisoner in Buchenwald concentration camp, taught Marxist philosophy. (After the foundation of the GDR he became the first secretary of state of higher education.) Albert Schreiner came from New York to accept the chair for "state science" and international relations. The head of the Leipzig city administration, Erich Zeigner, an old social democrat who had been head of the Saxon government deposed by the military in 1923, taught communal government as honorary professor.

Until the summer of 1949 the teaching staff was joined by other returning émigrés, among them Karl Polak (constitutional and state law) from the Soviet Union, Ernst Engelberg (history of the German labour movement) from Turkey, Hans Mayer (cultural history) from Switzerland, and Hermann Budzislawski (newspaper history and media technique), editor of the anti-Nazi journal *Neue Weltbühne* in Prague after 1934 and influential adviser and ghost-writer of the famous journalist Dorothy Thompson in New York during the war. Henryk Grossmann, a noted authority on political economy also came

8

from the United States. A Polish Jew by origin, he had lost his wife and his daughter in the Holocaust.

Professors from other faculties who had come to Leipzig lectured for us, too. Foremost among these were Werner Krauss, a notable scholar of Romance literature sentenced to death during the war and Julius Lips, an internationally well-known ethnologist of social democratic antecedents who had returned from the United States and was appointed Rector of the university in 1949. Another well respected scholar, whose lectures on legal and constitutional history were attended by a number of us, was the old liberal Erwin Jacobi, dismissed from the university after 1933 as a "half-Jew", who succeeded the philosopher Gadamer as Rector late in 1947 after the latter had "gone west". More important than these three was for us a brilliant young lecturer who had come from Bonn University and was destined for fame: the historian Walter Markov who had spent 10 years in prison under the Nazi regime. He taught world, German and Russian history, and was appointed professor in 1948.

Among the numerous guest lecturers invited by Hans Mayer, two were internationally famous: Bertolt Brecht and Hanns Eisler. The renowned poet and dramatist who had been given a theatre all for himself in East Berlin by our authorities, turned out to be an extremely poor speaker: his lecture consisted of monosyllabic reluctantly given answers to students' questions. Mayer tried very hard to get more out of him, but without success. Eisler, probably the greatest revolutionary composer of our century, a small, fattish and bald man whose appearance suggested a bank manager or shopkeeper, spoke about his encounters with the Senate Committee on Un-American activities in Washington and his experiences as professor at the Academy of Music in Chicago. The talents of some of his most gifted but penniless pupils, he said, had been ruined by their being forced to play every night in a jazz band – a fact which of course impressed his listeners.

During the three and a half years I spent at Leipzig University I went to the lectures and seminars of all those mentioned here and a few others from whom I learnt less. Since Schreiner and Markov were the academic teachers to whom I remained most indebted, I should say more about them.

The former (b. 1892) came from a working class family and was originally a goldsmith by trade. As a young man he joined the socialist youth movement and came under the influence of Clara Zetkin. Although an active opponent of the first world war he was promoted to the rank of cadet lieutenant before the war ended. It was, I suppose, because of his rank that he (at the age of 26!) became minister of war for a short time in the revolutionary government of Württemberg in 1918. In the KPD, which he helped to found in Stuttgart, he became the foremost military specialist, commanding operations during the Hamburg rising of 1923 and later as one of the leaders of the military organisation RFB. Later in the 1920s he was one of the editors of the collected works of Franz Mehring, the founder of German Marxist historiography. Expelled from the KPD in 1928 as an adherent of the right wing opposition, he was none the less compelled to emigrate to Paris in 1933, where he published a book on Hitler's preparation for war. Two years later he rejoined the KPD, going to Spain after the outbreak of war there to become chief of staff of the XIIIth International Brigade and then commander of a division of the republican army.

In 1938 he returned to Paris to write another book *Vom totalen Krieg zur totalen Niederlage Hitlers* ("From total war to Hitler's total defeat") in which he demonstrated that a German debacle in the imminent war would finally be inevitable. Interned after the war had begun, he managed to escape to the United States in 1941. There he was one of the founders of the Council for a Democratic Germany and published a book and various articles on German history. When he came to Leipzig in September 1947 I attached myself to him, since the chair of international relations seemed to offer what interested me most. He lectured mainly on the origins of the world wars since 1871 to students grateful for an outline of that subject from a Marxist point of view. Since he had no academic credentials he was at first somewhat nervous about his reception at the university, but his inaugural lecture was a complete success. Even the doyen of Saxon historians, Professor Kötzschke, attended. A little later Schreiner asked me to act as his assistant, which I agreed to knowing that he needed some help, that I could learn more in such a position, and that I would thus augment my stipend. He was not always easy to deal with, being sometimes charming but at other times distinctly quarrelsome and unapproachable, and my job as assistant obliged me on more than one occasion to pour oil on troubled waters. But I have every reason to be grateful to him since he taught me the methods of spadework in history and encouraged me to specialise in the history of colonialism.

Walter Markov, being younger (b. 1909), can be dealt with more briefly. Of German-Slovenian, middle-class origin, he had studied history, geography, philosophy and other subjects before being arrested in Bonn in 1935 as member of a group of student KPD sympathizers. Sentenced to 12 years' imprisonment, he organised an uprising in his prison when American troops approached it ten years later. In 1946 he moved to Leipzig, to become a lecturer and in 1948 professor of history. His lively, stimulating lectures and unassuming manner soon gained him great popularity.

Equipped with a truly stupendous store of historical knowledge he was often able to lecture without any preparation, or only with the aid of a few notes he had made on his shirt cuffs while travelling to the university. Knowing that he had little time to prepare (he also lectured at the neighbouring university of Halle) I sometimes waited for him outside the lecture hall, where he would always greet me with the question: "Tell me, where did I get to last time?". He made a habit of encouraging and sometimes leading discussions on such subjects as "Trotsky in 1917 " or Burnham's "manager theory" at that time popular with some anti-Marxists. In later years he was to become famous, being described by a French president as one of the three foremost authorities on the French Revolution.

The students of the faculty were, like the professors, untypical, many of them having (in accordance with their own wishes) been recommended by various branches of the SED, trade unions, the Liberal Democratic Party, the government of Saxony etc. Some of them had an anti-Nazi past. About a dozen had been members of communist or other resistance groups within Germany until 1945, more than double that number were former émigrés from Britain, the Soviet Union, Palestine, Sweden and other countries. At least five had served in the Allied forces during the war (one as captain in a British infantry regiment). One had deserted from the German army to the Soviet forces, another to a French underground resistance unit, several to the Greek liberation army. Another dozen or so had come from left wing organisations or universities in western Germany. At least two thirds of the faculty's students were members of the SED. Nearly all of them were politically motivated and for this reason worked hard.

Perhaps one fifth were aged between 30 and 40, a few were even older. Many of them came from working class families and did not have the kind of education needed for university studies. I will never forget the bewildered faces of a whole row of them as they listened to a lecture by Professor Gadamer: they did not understand a word. Those of us who had already studied at other universities or who had been teachers therefore founded a "studies commission" which organised help in various forms. We gave individual advice and instruction, wrote and printed lecture scripts and summaries, mimeographed excerpts from standard literature and distributed them. Sometimes, when serious difficulties arose, we intervened with the professor concerned. These activities certainly strengthened the morale of the weaker students; they cost the commission members quite a lot of time, however. Only seven of our students failed to pass the exams at the end of the first year; a few others gave up. Cases of indiscipline or immorality were usually dealt with by the party organisation. A married student was, for instance, told off in no uncertain terms for having a love affair with an unmarried girl; two others were severely reprimanded for having sold American cigarettes in Leipzig, which they had bought on the black market in Berlin. One was expelled, since it turned out that in his application to the university he had stated that he had studied theatre science at Königsberg during the war. Königsberg having been incorporated in the Soviet Union made it impossible to check this but unfortunately for him one of the members of our commission knew that this rare discipline (peculiar to Germany before 1945, if I am not mistaken) had never been taught there. The student in question, a former baker's apprentice who had wanted to make himself appear more acceptable, disappeared in a westerly direction, as for years to come almost everyone did who got into trouble.

I felt quite happy with the Gewifa. The atmosphere among the students was fraternal, optimistic, and usually harmonious; there was almost no infighting. They came to accept me and tolerated my British idiosyncrasies, such as avoiding the constant handshaking customary among Germans, or not greeting acquaintances I saw on the other side of the street. Only once a female student shouted at me indignantly when I did not greet her, leaving me rather embarrassed. But I only changed my ways very slowly.

Since the summer of 1947 the policy of making it easier for young people from the working class to enter universities began to arouse the opposition of middle class students (the upper class had virtually disappeared in 1945). The SED rightly thought it impossible to erect the stable new democracy it was aiming at without training large numbers of young workers as teachers, managers, civil engineers, doctors, civil servants and so on. In the universities this policy was justified, inter alia, with the argument that all parts of the population had a claim to be represented more or less according to their relative numerical strength. Such ideas were, understandably, regarded by many professional people with an academic background as an attack on the chances of their children and as smacking of socialism. Their sons at the universities, backed by the Liberal Democratic Party, saw it the same way. At a students' meeting I went to one day, a student protested that while formerly an Aryan grandmother was needed to enter the university, now a proletarian grandmother was required.

Another in the course of a lengthy diatribe said that if all parts of the population had a claim to be represented, the 5 per cent half-wits should be included. One of our students, who came from a Berlin trade union, interrupted him excitedly and shouted that he felt himself insulted. He called on all working class students present to leave the meeting in protest. Of course, as a socialist I joined those who left and gathered in the lecture hall next door. There, amid general indignation and confusion, a female student of Markov's and I wrote a resolution in favour of working class admission. It was put to the vote, agreed to unanimously and sent to the Rector.

This conflict went on for months, with the executive committee of the university's student union, in which members of the Liberal Democratic and Christian Democratic parties were in the majority, taking sides against us. At a students' meeting in the largest hall in Leipzig, one of the trade unions leaders in Saxony, Jahn, appealed to the hundreds present to support the ending of the discrimination against workers in education. He argued that this was essential for the new democracy, but was shouted down.

The conflict broke off abruptly in a way I did not like much. The chairman of the students' union, Natonek, and some members of the executive committee were arrested by the Soviet authorities because, as a curt notice in the local newspaper stated, they had been in touch with United States agencies. Not that the accusation was prima facie improbable: the Cold War was now in full blast and parts of what remained of the middle class in Leipzig were clearly looking to the United States for salvation. (When travelling from my lodgings in the south west of Leipzig to the university in the centre I often saw fur traders and other well-dressed people furtively reading the Tagesspiegel, a newspaper published in West Berlin under American auspices.) The students arrested in Leipzig were not, to my knowledge, put on trial but released after some time. Many of their supporters left the town in the following months and continued their studies at universities in the West. Without the arrests the conflict would have come to an end a little later with this "emigration" in any case.

The conflict at Leipzig and a similar one at Berlin University at the same time were the last cases of open political opposition to the policies of the SED in the Soviet Zone and the Soviet sector of Berlin until 17 June 1953. From now on opposition took the form of complaint and agitation at a private level, and sometimes sabotage in industry. It was much encouraged by the American radio station RIAS from West Berlin. People who strongly disagreed with the Soviet administration and the SED packed their bags and moved to the Western zones, where these "emigrants" were increasingly aided by the authorities and various non-official bodies.

But most people leaving for the West now went because living conditions were obviously improving there, whereas progress in the Soviet Zone in 1947-8, though perceptible, was much slower. They thought that their business or career prospects in the Soviet Zone were dim. For instance, the husband of my landlady, director of a factory for chocolate products, had gone off with his secretary to found another factory in the West. Nearly everyone had relations in West Germany or knew people who had gone there.

In the summer of 1947 there was almost nothing to be had on ration cards in Leipzig except some bread and poor quality meat. A brilliant assistant of Werner Krauss who had come from a university in West Germany to work with him, stuck it out for some months but then capitulated and went back. My body weight went down from almost 70 kilos to less than 50 kilos, with the result that my appearance shocked my mother and friends when I went home to Berlin in the summer holidays of 1948.

In that summer, after regaining my normal weight, I spent 3 weeks in Bonn, Cologne and Hildesheim near Hanover, all in the British Zone, visiting my grandmother and various aunts and uncles. Although food was still rationed, no one seemed to lack the goods needed for daily subsistence. There was quite a lot of building and of restoration of war ruins going on; obviously American investment and loans were beginning to give the economy a boost. The appearance of many products on sale, of new motorways, of cars and many other things was more American than German. It was obvious that the Western powers, especially the United States, were building up Western and Southern Germany as a barrier against "Communism".

Developments in all parts of Germany in 1948 were mainly dictated by the Cold War. The Western powers decided to turn their three zones into a new German state. With this aim in view they introduced a new currency in their zones in June 1948 and included these zones in the Marshall Plan in the following months. After they had officially declared their assent to the foundation of the West German state and thus to the long-term separation of Germany in April 1949 a federal parliament was elected in August which constituted itself on 7 September in Bonn.

A week later it chose Konrad Adenauer as Chancellor of the Federal Republic of Germany. He was well-known as a right-wing Catholic politician, who in the Weimar Republic before 1933 had steered a conservative and anti-democratic course. He had taken no part in the resistance against the Hitler regime and saw no reason why he should not appoint one of the bureaucratic architects of the Holocaust, Globke, to the position of Secretary of State in the Federal Chancellor's office, i.e. as his highest ranking aide.

My friends, fellow students and I viewed this whole chain of events with deep apprehension. All of us who had taken some part, however modest and junior, in resistance to the Hitler regime were deeply convinced of the vital need to ensure beyond a shadow of doubt that Germany never again dragged humanity into war. My father and three of my émigré friends had given their lives in the struggle against that regime. The agreement concluded by the Allies at Potsdam in 1945 had been intended to guarantee the transformation of Germany into a democracy, its de-nazification and demilitarisation. And what had happened? In 1945-6 the Western allies took a number of steps to implement that agreement, but since then had deviated increasingly from it. In the Soviet Zone the police, judiciary and entire administration of the Nazi regime had been dissolved, their members being excluded from public service (the only exception being the staff of land register offices). School teachers who had been members of the Nazi party were dismissed; Nazis who had committed crimes were arrested and put on trial.

I was present at two such trials in Leipzig as a spectator. The accused in one case was a police informer who had denounced a number of his neighbours in a Leipzig working-class district as opponents of the Hitler regime. He was a cringing creature, a human worm, and was sentenced to only three years in prison, because, it seemed to me, some of the witnesses obviously exaggerated his misdeeds. The other case was far worse. About thirty employees of a factory producing textiles were charged with absolutely shocking ill-treatment of Russian and Polish prisoners handed over to their firm for unskilled labour. The prisoners had been constantly beaten, locked up for days without food etc., and so on; some had even been beaten to death by the accused, who all looked like average, normal man-in-the-street types of Germans. About half of them had to be acquitted because of insufficient evidence of their personal guilt; the others were given stiff sentences. The directors of the firm had of course gone West, and no Nazi in West Germany was ever handed over to an East German court of justice.

In the Soviet Zone no person who had been a member of the Nazi party could hold a position of authority, with the exception of a small number of doctors, distinguished scientists, and highly qualified engineers. A very few exceptions were made for people for whom membership had been a cover for resistance. As for the economy, all enterprises belonging to Nazi or war criminals – which in practice meant virtually all large and many medium-sized firms – were confiscated by the Soviet military administration in 1945 and, except for some provisionally retained as reparations, turned over to the new provincial administrations in the following year. In many areas the new local German authorities had by this time on their own initiative taken over works deserted by their former owners and, as far as possible, begun manufacturing much needed consumer goods.

Agricultural estates of more than two hectares (247 acres), except for church property, had in 1945 been divided into small plots of 0.5 to 10 hectares and given over to about half-a-million new owners: Germans from eastern provinces taken over by Poland and from other East European countries, agricultural labourers who had worked on the partitioned estates, small farmers, and other applicants.

But the Soviet Zone, where Nazism had been radically destroyed, comprised only one third of what had remained of Germany. It conspicuously lacked raw materials, except for lignite and some agricultural products such as sugar-beet. Two thirds of its natural capital, Berlin, were occupied by powers that had become increasingly hostile. About one half of its population had relations, old friends or other connections in the other part of Germany. For all these and other reasons, it was obviously going to be very difficult to ensure that the direction Germany took would not resemble the course that had led to two world wars.

It was obvious that the Soviet Union and the leaders of the SED would have to react to the creation of a three-zone West German state, even if that state was at first far from being independent.

Their answer was to turn the Soviet Zone into the German Democratic Republic, although such a step had not been intended and preparations had not been made.

On 7 October 1949 at midday the party organisation at the university called on all members to come to the Karl-Marx-Platz in the centre of Leipzig in the evening. When we arrived we found that on the west side of the square a high platform had been erected. On it were sitting the second secretary of the Leipzig SED, Erich Richter, leading figures of the other parties, the trades unions and some people we did not know. At eight o'clock Richter stepped to the microphone and told the audience, about one thousand strong, that the People's Council in Berlin (a coalition of all parties and other important organisations) had on that day proclaimed the German Democratic Republic, so that we now had our own state. He was not an impressive speaker and I have forgotten the rest of his speech. Anyway, we all cheered, understanding that an important decision had been taken. The meeting left the impression of having been improvised.

In the side streets a few people had without success attempted to turn back those going to the meeting. Except for this there was, as far as I know, no sign of opposition. But the news was not received with acclaim either. A widespread attitude was: we are a conquered people and the occupants will decide on our future. The population received the news passively, although some people clung to the idea of a united Germany. I suppose that most people had no clear idea of the consequences. The general feeling in western and southern Germany about the founding of the Federal Republic seems to have been similar. There were no jubilant crowds on the streets there either.

The handing over of full authority to the German provincial governments and administrations in the Soviet Zone followed gradually. At first one noticed little change.

Our new government did not accept separation as a long-term aim, but strove with unrelenting political and propagandist efforts for a united demilitarised Germany based on the principles of the Potsdam Agreement. A great youth rally in support of this policy took place in Berlin in the summer of 1950, which I remember as an exhilarating and at the same time exhausting event. About one year before the initially small organisation of the Free German Youth in the university had been founded and, following an appeal by the local SED, all students who were party members had joined. In practice this did not mean much, and those of us who were really too old for any youth movement did not take it seriously. But when the great youth rally approached we were all mobilised. We had to appear at local rallies dressed in blue shirts with the insignia of the organisation and patiently listen to harangues by local youth leaders. When they demanded that we rehearse marching in closed formations there was trouble; quite a few students had been soldiers in Hitler's army and had a deep revulsion against anything smacking of military service. They only reluctantly agreed to carry on with the rehearsal after prolonged and heated discussions.

But when we were marching to Berlin the old instinctive urge for mechanical uniformity (stronger among Germans, it seems, than among most nations) asserted itself. Since the sun was strong I was wearing a beret which I kept on when others took off their headwear. Finally I was the only one in the whole column with something on his head. Soon grumbling began behind me and then a chorus shouted "Stoecker, take that cap off!" Since I took no notice and no one intervened the shouting went on for about half an hour and then suddenly ceased. I wondered whether this could have happened in a British or French youth organisation, but did not take it very seriously, except for one lesson: never to give way to stupid demands for uniformity unless the price of refusal was higher than the issue at stake seemed to justify. We reached Berlin aboard a goods train, which shunted around for many hours before unloading us near the Nordbahnhof where, tired out, we spent the night on heaps of straw. The rally itself was enjoyable. Large numbers of young people from various parts of Germany took part.

The most important of the many subjects being discussed among students of our faculty about this time was the nature of the society being built up in the GDR. At first the SED, represented by Anton Ackermann, had advocated a "special German road to socialism" on which the "new democracy" created since 1945 was to be the first step. Later Georgi Dimitrov put forward the concept of "People's Democracy" as a stage of transition to socialism in the eastern and central European countries liberated by Soviet armies or their own liberation movements (Yugoslavia, Albania) in 1944/1945. It was the latter formula which was turned over and over in our discussions. Some ridiculed it as pompous nonsense and pointed out that linguistically it was a tautology since "demos" in any case meant "people". The majority, however, (to which, in this case, I belonged) supported the idea, not necessarily the term, and some of us searched, without success, for a better formulation. Our society was obviously fundamentally different from the social order of the Federal Republic, where the ruling class of Nazi Germany and its upper middle class, with the exception of a few professional Nazis, were engaged in holding or regaining their former positions. In this they had the tacit support of the Western powers. The economy of the Federal Republic was fully capitalist.

In the Soviet Zone, now the GDR, positions of economic, social or political influence had been more and more taken over by people belonging to the working class and, to some extent, the lower middle class and the peasantry. Economically and politically the power of the former ruling class had been destroyed. But the economy was not socialist. Agriculture was predominantly in the hands of small, medium and wealthy farmers, industry was in parts being run by local authorities or other state bodies as "people's own", but a high proportion of the small and medium-sized enterprises were in private hands. An important part of industry, at first scheduled to be transported to the Soviet Union as reparations, was being run under Soviet control as Soviet property. Trade was partly carried on by cooperative societies but to a great extent was in private hands. Banks and insurance were being run by directors provisionally appointed by the new state. Landed property had not been expropriated, except for large estates, and housing had mainly remained private property, too. To find an accurate formula for this state of affairs was, of course, difficult indeed, and it is no wonder that our attempts failed.

In the summer of 1949 Bernhard Steinberger, until 1945 a refugee in Switzerland, who was Professor Behrens' assistant, suddenly disappeared. After a few days we heard that he and his Hungarian wife had been arrested by the Soviet authorities. Nothing was published about the arrest, which we conjectured might have been due to the connections of his wife to László Rajk and his comrades in Budapest. Thus the tragic affair of Rajk had cast its shadows as far as Leipzig University. As for the Steinbergers we did not believe that they were American agents, but we trusted the Soviet authorities. That our trust had been misplaced became evident only after Stalin's death, when the Steinbergers were released and declared innocent. The news of arrests in Prague and then of the few such cases in the GDR puzzled us, of course. I remember an intense and moving discussion between half a dozen students who were former émigrés. A young woman broke down in tears after exclaiming that she could not bear the suspicion with which former refugees from Nazism who had returned from the western countries were being regarded. The rest of us calmed her, pointing out that only a tiny number had been arrested or dismissed from responsible positions. (Of course we did not know that all such former "West emigrants" were to be excluded from state service and the army later.) We realised that under the conditions of the Cold War, in which the Americans were known to be spending enormous sums on espionage and sabotage in Eastern Europe, there must be U.S. agents at work in our republic. But should these be looked for among former refugees from Nazism, whose identity and record could as a rule easily be checked? Former Nazis and resettlers from now Polish provinces seemed far more likely suspects.

The prevailing opinion was that one had to trust the Soviets and our own security people, whether their actions were comprehensible or not. "The party may make mistakes, but it will always correct them sooner or later" was a deep-seated attitude. Nonetheless disagreement and disgust among those affected continued.

When I visited a trusted friend, Siegbert Kahn, who was director of an institute of economic research in East Berlin, he made no bones about his discontent, exclaiming "Under the Nazis I was a Jew, in England I was an enemy alien, and now I am a West emigrant".

But I do not remember a single case in which the odium cast on "West Emigrants" in those years led to those affected leaving the GDR. Attachment to the GDR and rejection of the Federal Republic were far too strong for such a step, which would have been unthinkable for me and other former émigrés I knew.

This sad chapter ended in Leipzig with the wholly unjustified expulsion of Walter Markov from the SED. The local party newspaper surprised us considerable one day by accusing him of being a "Titoist agent", whatever that might have been. The party organisation opened disciplinary proceedings against him. A few weeks later the Central Party Control Commission sent a representative to Leipzig to clear up the affair. This man consulted the city secretariat of the SED and then took the unusual step of asking Markov and five or six of us who knew him well to meet him for a discussion. Some of those who took part avoided taking Markov's side, although they must have known that the accusation was ridiculous, which annoyed me very much. When my turn came to speak I declared heatedly that Markov was being unjustly accused and that there was no reason for any proceedings. The only charge which could be put forward against him was that he had invited a writer of doubtful qualifications and possibly connected with British intelligence to give us a guest lecture on a subject without political significance. Markov bore all this with outward equanimity, but I am certain that he was deeply wounded and indignant.

In the upshot Markov was expelled from the party but not from the university. This result was to benefit him and the university greatly, since he saved much time in the following decades by not having to take part in any party activities and being able to concentrate entirely on his work. It was the only time I had been drawn into this appalling chapter of party and GDR history, initiated and enforced by Soviet leaders who disappeared from the political stage a few years later after having compromised the cause they were supposed to represent to a degree for which the term "unforgivable" is hopelessly inadequate. The fact that the GDR was the least affected among the Soviet Union's closer allies was no consolation.

When I left Leipzig after taking my finals in October/November 1950 the situation there had changed for the better but was still far from satisfactory. The conditions of near-starvation had been overcome. Rations had been increased and it was now possible to buy food, textiles and other goods freely at state shops. Housing conditions remained extremely bad however, especially in the working class districts. Most prisoners-of-war had returned home, bringing the labour situation nearer to normal. The SED, the trade unions and the Free German Youth were gaining influence. More and more people were in one way or another being drawn into the voluntary activities devoted to rebuilding the country. Clearing the streets of the rubble still lying around and salvaging bricks from ruined buildings so that they could be used again became a weekend occupation for many people for several years. (Our Gewifa students gave a good example here.)

It was also noticeable that members of the professional, intellectual and artistic stratum were realising that the new order had come to stay, for the time being at least, and that they could play a part in it. Many of these people came to understand that there was such a thing as Russian or Soviet culture which should be taken notice of. Lectures and performances at the House of Soviet Culture, opened in 1949 by the Soviet Military Administration, were well attended, as was Gorky's Mother at the city theatre. Soviet officers gave public lectures in German. Of these I particularly remember lectures on Marxist philosophy given by a Major Patent, in civil life a university lecturer, which were so popular that Leipzig's largest meeting hall was not big enough to hold the audience.

Berlin 1951 – 52.
Living in East Berlin from December 1950, I took up work as an assistant editor in the foreign news department of the GDR news agency ADN early the following year. This official agency which cooperated with TASS and Reuters, supplied all GDR newspapers and radio stations with news, leaders, commentaries and articles. It had correspondents in all the larger towns of the GDR, but in those early years almost none outside its borders. It therefore derived its news from abroad almost solely from TASS and Reuters and to a smaller extent from foreign newspapers and news bulletins recorded by stenographers from broadcasts. The work of the editorial staff of the foreign news department consisted mainly in adapting the news received from TASS and

Reuters in the radio transmitter's rooms in Russian or English into items for German consumption. This raw material we were given was usually translated into bad or faulty German before it reached us, and we were supposed to edit and write it up, sometimes supplementing it by news drawn from newspapers from West Berlin, Paris or London. Whatever we produced went on the table of the acting editor-in-chief, who either sent it on to the transmission rooms or gave it back to us for changes he wanted. That this method of running a news service was fraught with all sorts of risks was obvious, and the quality of news from abroad published in the GDR at this time was hardly impeccable. The journalists working for ADN in 1951 were a mixed lot. On the one hand there were quite a number of convinced communists and socialists (not all members of the SED) among them, doing their difficult job as well as they could. The best were men and women such as the director Georg Hansen, an old communist who had worked on Radio Moscow during the war; Max Kahane, deputy director, who had fought in the French resistance; Fritz Teppich, a Jew from West Berlin who had somehow survived the Holocaust; and my special friend Ruth Hirsch who had returned to Berlin from Palestine because she was disillusioned with Zionism.

On the other hand, there were not a few – to my surprise partly residents of West Berlin – who had no serious convictions of any kind and wrote as they thought ADN wanted them to simply because they were fairly well paid. In the Berlin department there were even people who had worked for the Goebbels press. Others were former schoolteachers who had been dismissed from their profession because they had been members of the Nazi party (these were normally harmless but not much good as journalists). Between the two categories mentioned there were people whose integrity was evident but who stopped short of any political affiliation, such as an excellent editor at the foreign news department who was a Baptist.

When I entered ADN it had not yet overcome the instability typical of many institutions of the Soviet Zone in the first post-war years. The chief reporter had just deserted to the West and was publishing a sensational series about his experiences in the London *Daily Express*. At the first party meeting I took part in, the head of the German department was drummed out of the party and ADN for being frequently drunk when he should have been working and for not paying back large sums he had borrowed from his colleagues. A few months later the party secretary, an extremely primitive and stupid individual, was arrested and sentenced to 5 years imprisonment. He had for some time been selling copies of his monthly routine reports on party activities in ADN to American intelligence.

I soon found out that the work at the foreign news department was not to my taste. When I accidentally met the director and he asked me how I liked my new job I replied that writing reports about men biting dogs was not the kind of task that could make me happy. He laughed and said that if I would carry on a little longer, he would have a better position for me. A couple of months later I was called to his secretariat. So much faulty or mistaken news and articles were being sent out by the various departments that it had been decided to have an additional control by three young editors of everything sent out. I was to be one of these and accepted the arrangement. We worked in 3 shifts round the clock, sorting out items we thought faulty. These were sent back to the department responsible or, if we were uncertain, submitted to the director or his deputy. It turned out that we seldom had political objections to the innumerable items we had to countersign, but frequently discovered errors or faults resulting from slipshod work. The only department we never collided with was that for sports news. But our control did not prevent a gaffe regarded as simply awful: one night ADN sent out a speech of Stalin's which came too late for most newspapers but was printed in the later editions of a few. It then turned out that the speech had not been given by Stalin at all but by one Skalin, unknown to the world at large. The second letter of the speaker's name had been missing at the head in the transmitted text, and the operator, jumping to conclusions, had filled the gap with the letter "t". He was sacked on the spot and an apology broadcast.

After about two months my reading, just scanning or simply glancing at the products of the various departments came to an end. The directors were justly dissatisfied with the quality of the staff at the Berlin office, but there was, it seemed, little chance of recruiting other journalists anywhere. Therefore they decided to train very young candidates for the profession within the firm. Kahane, the personnel manager Kempf (a former police officer whose health had been badly damaged by imprisonment in Buchenwald concentration camp) and I travelled together around the GDR to interview young people between 17 and 19 years of age who had been nominated by the branch managers. The idea was to turn as many of them as possible into assistant editors or reporters within two years at the most. We selected twenty two who were housed in a hostel in Strausberg near Berlin and put in my charge. (It was symptomatic of conditions at that time that I had to ask them to bring pillows along, because we had none and could not obtain any.) I was to organise their training, presumably because I was the only member of the staff who had a university degree and a little experience in teaching. Getting this scheme under way was to be my task during the second half of 1951.

This sort of thing was of course more to my liking than journalistic drudgery. I worked out a curriculum, which was approved with some alterations by the directors. Then I engaged teachers for typewriting, shorthand, journalistic practice, geography, German, Russian and English.

World History in the 20th century I taught myself. Lessons in German were needed because instruction in that subject in the schools was – and continued to be – unsatisfactory. A few weeks after the arrival of the trainees in July, the courses were under way. With the trainees I had few difficulties. I liked them and I don't think they disliked me. Kahane and Kempf had told me that the scheme would be worthwhile even if only six or seven of the young people could later be employed by ADN, and therefore the demands I made of them were not small. With the support of some party members among them I encouraged help by the more advanced for the weaker ones, as had been practised by Gewifa students in Leipzig. Only two trainees had dropped out by the end of the year when I left ADN. One of these had been accused at a meeting of the trainees of spending his nights with prostitutes and thereupon decided to leave; the other, by pretending to be a doctor, had obtained samples of medicines free of charge from a West German firm. He was dismissed.

On the whole the course was a success. Several trainees became first-rate journalists in later years: two were for a long time correspondents in Paris, another served ADN in Cairo and Baghdad, others in Warsaw, Stockholm and so on. One was to become a well-known author of science fiction novels, another eventually published books for children. While working for ADN I joined a small pool of former émigrés who with the permission of their employers from time to time acted as interpreters and translators at international conferences or for foreign visitors. These occasions were usually strenuous and not particularly interesting, but two trips I made as an interpreter are perhaps worth mentioning. One was with about a dozen participants in an international peace symposium from Britain, India and Senegal, who travelled through Mecklenburg in a bus, speaking at meetings and receptions. Interpreting without a pause for sixteen hours and more daily was of course a great strain, but it was worth it: the travellers in that bus were very much impressed and touched by the friendliness and sympathy with which they were received by everyone from the ministers of the provincial government of Mecklenburg to the last schoolchild. They left tired but convinced that the people of the GDR backed the struggle for peace enthusiastically. And the people they had spoken to had received an impression of the world-wide and varied character of that struggle.

The other was a week's trip through Brandenburg and Sachsen-Anhalt as interpreter for the elderly wife of an Australian high-court judge, also guest of the Peace Council. She just wanted to look around and talk to people, especially in agriculture. In Brandenburg most villages looked poor, ugly and depressing, but this was the result of centuries of extreme exploitation, not of "new democracy" or the land reform. Sachsen-Anhalt on the whole offered a better picture, but here villagers often worked in industry.

The peasants we spoke with were all more or less content with their lot, whether they had inherited their farms from their fathers or had received their land only a few years before when the large estates were divided up. If they were not content they did not say so, but their situation was obviously better than that of most city dwellers. One large village was a special case. The inhabitants were German workers, "re-settlers" from Czechoslovakia who, as firm communists, had founded an agricultural cooperative, a kolkhoz on the Soviet model. The local SED leaders had their doubts since this went far beyond the directives from the Central Committee, but tolerated it since it functioned well. This village made an exceptionally good impression. Everything was very clean and the people there looked happy and were obviously proud of what they had achieved. They were interested in world affairs and were the only ones we met who asked questions about Australia.

After my finals I had chosen journalism because newspapers had always interested me. At the age of sixteen, I had carefully measured out a copy of the Daily Express to find out how much of it consisted of advertisements. Then I read several books about Britain's newspapers to find out why they had been founded and what purposes they served. What I had learnt about Northcliffe and Beaverbrook was later in Leipzig supplemented by Budzislawski's lectures on media history. But soon after entering ADN I realised that I had made a serious mistake; not only the foreign news department but journalism in general were spheres which could never really satisfy me. I hated writing against the clock. Scholarship, I came to realise, was the field in which I could best put to use whatever abilities I might have. A political career would also have been thinkable but I strongly doubted if my nature would stand the strain of constant disputes and a life largely filled out with committee meetings and never-ending sessions – a vice highly developed in Germany – and much more subject to party discipline as interpreted by party secretaries and committees.

Alfred Meusel whom I went to see invited me to his lectures at the university on the English Revolution of the seventeenth century, as far as my duties at ADN permitted, and to take part in his monthly seminar for young historians preparing doctoral theses. This was an honour indeed: Meusel was at that time the leading historian of the GDR and the participants were a select company. A little later he suggested that I begin work on a PhD thesis, too. He readily agreed that the subject should be "German relations with China in the 19th century", which Schreiner in Leipzig had already encouraged me to explore.

Meusel was to play an important part in my life during the next few years. Born in Kiel in 1896 as son of a high-ranking civil servant, he had been a student at Kiel University when the First World War began. As a young infantry officer he had been seriously wounded on the western front, being buried alive by a shell in a trench during an enemy attack. Because of his injuries he was for the rest of his life handicapped by a slight nervous impediment of speech but this did not prevent him from becoming a brilliant lecturer in later years. His experiences in the war turned him into a deeply convinced opponent of the whole imperialist regime in Germany. After he had been found unfit for further military service and resumed his studies in his native city, he joined the Independent Social Democratic Party and acted as chairman of the students' socialist group in Kiel. His exceptional academic attainments led to his being appointed professor of sociology at Aachen at the age of only twenty nine.

In the 1920s and early 1930s he belonged to no party but was chairman of the local branch of the Friends of the Soviet Union. Well-known in Aachen as an active left-winger, he was forced to emigrate to Denmark in 1933 and was then engaged as a research worker by a British sociological institute. In London he founded the "Friends of the German People's Front" in 1938 and in the following year, with other prominent émigrés, the "Free German League of Culture". Meusel and the philosopher Arthur Liebert were the leading spirits of the "Free German High School", where his lectures on modern German history (which I attended) found many enthusiastic listeners. On coming to Berlin in 1946 he was appointed professor of modern history at the Humboldt University. In December 1951 a small working group which, under Meusel's chairmanship, was preparing the foundation of a museum of

German history in Berlin offered me a position as assistant. I was glad to accept and in January began work in the museum, where I was placed in the department dealing with the era 1917-1945. The head of the department was Schreiner.

Ironically enough, four of the eight members of the department were former émigrés from western countries (USA, England, Switzerland) who were also strongly represented in other departments. Suspect "West Emigrants" were thus in charge of an essential part of the "ideological front" (an expression used humorously within party circles). The approximately seventy people who were to create the museum were provisionally placed in a building behind the university, formerly used as a school for librarians. This building was to house the first exhibition too, for the much larger *Zeughaus* (armoury of the kings of Prussia) which was to be its domicile, had been badly damaged in air raids and had to be rebuilt before it could be moved into. The academic staff were largely drawn from the Humboldt University. As for exhibits we had to start almost from scratch for the only significant source we could draw on immediately was the huge collection of weapons and armour formerly shown in the Zeughaus which had luckily survived the war. We roved around in search of materials which could illustrate our era: documents from various archives, books and journals from libraries, photos and works of art.

I knew that the guillotine with which the Nazis had executed at least 1,500 political prisoners in Brandenburg prison was still there, and my proposal to acquire it was accepted by Meusel. After the Ministry of the Interior had agreed I was sent to the prison to negotiate the transport. It was a large, modern building, in which several hundred men were serving long sentences for Nazi and war crimes. After I had passed a strict control, the director gave me a friendly reception. He introduced himself as a veteran of the International Brigades in Spain and handed me over to an elderly officer who took me to the garage where the guillotine was which had been used to murder so many of the best men and women Germany had brought forth in our time, among them friends and associates of my father's whom I remembered. The officer, who had himself been a political prisoner in Brandenburg, explained how executions were carried out. The visit to this terrible site moved me deeply and even now, more than forty years later, I clearly remember every part of it. When the guillotine had been re-erected in our museum Schreiner asked Bert Brecht, with whom he was acquainted, to write a comment on it, which Brecht did. It was attached to the horrible instrument.

On another occasion I visited the painter Hans Grundig in his studio in a building of the former Academy of Arts in Dresden, to see if any of his works were of interest for us. This first-rate artist, who was obviously weakened by the tuberculosis he had contracted in a concentration camp, showed me a dozen pictures he had secretly painted after 1935. He made a resigned and somewhat melancholy impression, perhaps also because since the year before there had been severe criticism of "formalistic art" by party theoreticians. His paintings reflected his deep execration of the barbarity of Nazism and the inhumanity of war, but most of them were not easy to comprehend at first sight, because of the symbols he often employed. Nonetheless, I recommended several for acquisition by the museum. Schreiner at first showed little inclination to take them, saying that this excellent painter had, like many others, unfortunately been much influenced by expressionism, which the KPD had rejected for years. But finally Grundig's picture *Victims of Fascism* was bought and included in the museum's first exhibition, as were works by other anti-Nazi painters and sculptors such as Heinz Worner and Max Lingner.

It was the discovery of an exhibit of a very different kind that gave me some satisfaction. A few days after the German attack on the Soviet Union in 1941, one or two London newspapers had reported a speech by Harry S. Truman, who at that time was senator for Missouri and now, in 1952, President of the United States. He had declared that the more Germans and Russians killed each other, the better it would be for the United States. This must have been reported first by the U.S. newspapers, I thought, and some of these must have reached Berlin via Lisbon or Stockholm to be read in Berlin ministries and then deposited in their records. I therefore began searching for ministerial archives of those years, and after many days of fruitless labour finally succeeded, to the great surprise of Meusel, Schreiner and all my colleagues in finding a New York newspaper with the incriminating text in the cellar of a ruined building. It was put into a frame and hung up in a prominent place among pictures of Hitler's aggression of 1941. (It was about this time that Siegbert Kahn discovered and saved historically important records of the Deutsche Bank in another cellar, after absent-mindedly glancing at documents he was about to use as toilet paper in the lavatory above it.)

However, the search for exhibits was not the crucial task assigned to the museum staff. The scenarios the departments wrote as guidelines for the illustration of German history with carefully selected objects (many of which were copies, reproductions, maps or charts especially made for us) were also intended to be first, rough drafts of outlines to be used by the many institutions at which history was taught. Each draft on a certain period or subject was extensively discussed in the department responsible, revised, submitted to Meusel and the leading historians of the museum, discussed again, revised again, and so on. An active participant in these discussions was Ernst Diehl, chief historian of the Central Committee of the SED, who once inadvertently aroused much hilarity by speaking of the "readers of the museum"; the visitor was obviously going to be confronted by much more reading matter than exhibits to look at. Sometimes two prominent members of the Central Committee also took part. Fred Oelssner, an economist with a genuine interest in history, confined himself to general remarks and tried to be helpful; Kurt Hager, a philosopher who had been head of the organisation of the KPD in Britain in the later years of the war, irritated us by commenting in great detail on numerous matters. But these men from the Central Committee never tried to give us orders.

Marked differences of opinion on the character of the German revolution of 1918 between Meusel and Schreiner finally came to dominate these discussions. The former held that it was a bourgeois-democratic revolution, the latter that it was proletarian and socialist. Debates on this difficult problem were to continue for some years. Among us younger historians opinions tended more to Meusel's view, but most of us reserved judgement, being uncertain about it.

As for me, I took little part in these discussions, for the simple reason that I knew less than my colleagues about the period 1917-45, which had not been lectured on at Leipzig. And the tendency to depict German history as a succession of progressive movements led by progressive personalities increasingly irritated me. Had not Marx and Engels characterised German history in the nineteenth century as a "misére"? And had not Alexander Abusch in 1945 published his book *Irrweg einer Nation* (The Aberrant Road of a Nation)? Why was there no serious attempt to explain the loss of so much of Eastern Germany to Poland? And why was there no explanation of the fact that the majority of all Germans had followed Hitler until 1945?

I felt still worse about the disregard for some of the facts about the political biography of Ernst Thälmann. The unification of the left wing of the Independent Socialist Party and the KPD in 1920 did not take place under his leadership, as was asserted in our outline and the literature then being published on party history. Schreiner, who had worked together with Thälmann for a number of years, constantly refused to write or speak about his experiences. It was easy to understand the reason: he did not want to refute the image of a infallible hero that short-sighted propagandists were building up. Perhaps inner conflicts on matters such as this one were the reason for his recurring irritability, which made it more difficult than formerly to work with him.

My doubts and reservations did not mean that I rejected the attempt to re-write German history, although the foundation of a museum seemed a rather odd way of beginning such an enterprise. On the contrary: I supported it wholeheartedly. Seeing that in the Federal Republic many historians who had unscrupulously served the Nazi regime had returned to the universities and were training the new generation of students, that the literature published on German history there, with few exceptions, showed no signs of a democratic spirit, that there was, for example, no attempt critically to examine the traditional nationalist idealisation of Frederick II of Prussia or of Bismarck, the sorry role of German historians in the campaign against the "War Guilt Lie" after the first world war – in view of all this, an attempt at thorough historical revision in the GDR was obviously an inescapable moral and political obligation. It would have been unforgivable not to demolish the shibboleths of former German nationalist and expansionist historiography and not to expose the falsifications it had produced and propagated in such abundance.

The month of July 1952 saw a momentous decision. The "Second Party Conference" of the SED decided that the republic should proceed to "build socialism". As far as I remember, the decision did not arouse much interest in the party at the time. It was seen as the logical continuation of internal developments of which the main feature was gradual economic progress, although the after-effects of the war were still far from overcome. Huge new factories had been erected, wage levels had risen, prices in state shops had fallen. Agriculture was progressing too. The population in general paid little attention to the decision, since it had no effects on everyday life, which went on as usual. For many people it was a matter of no importance whether the unsatisfactory conditions they were living in were called "people's democracy" or "building socialism".

The foremost aim, which found very wide support, was the unification of Germany with a neutral status guaranteed by the four powers. Unfortunately this sensible idea was strictly rejected by Adenauer and the U.S. administration. In May the Chancellor had signed two treaties which firmly bound the Federal Republic to the Western Powers. There is no doubt that a neutralised Germany would have meant the end of the Cold War and a good foundation for durable peace in Europe, but the right wing politicians in the Federal Republic contemptuously described it as "Finlandisation".

The Soviet Union continued to strive for a neutralised united Germany till 1955, but was the decision of the SED to "build up socialism" really fully compatible with Soviet policy? It was, so it seems, a lone decision of the party leaders. It had neither been discussed by the party members nor in parliament. Even the Central Committee, confronted with it the day before the conference began, did not discuss it properly. Such a procedure would not, I feel certain, have been approved by Lenin. It showed the influence of Stalin's methods of leadership, which was to bedevil the GDR to its very end. The decision to "build up socialism" was not, as in Czechoslovakia in 1948, taken after large parts of the industrial working class had demanded it, but because the leaders thought it possible and opportune.

As for my friends, my colleagues at the museum and myself, we did not realize the full implications of beginning to "construct socialism" in the GDR. As socialists, we of course assented to the new strategy, but I do not remember any enthusiasm. Everyone was rather surprised. I felt doubts about Ulbricht's assertion that "the consciousness of the working class and the majority of the labouring people" were really ripe for such a step, but said to myself (as I was to do repeatedly in the years to come) that the party leadership was much better informed and experienced than I was and that it must know what it was doing. And the discipline now demanded from party members required outward acquiescence. That my doubts were justified was to become evident a year later.

The foundation of the GDR was a defensive act forced on Moscow and the SED, but there were no compelling reasons for Ulbricht's announcement in 1952. Soviet assent to this step was received in Berlin only one day before the party conference was opened and – which was unusual – no Soviet delegation took part. Historical research on the subject has not as yet provided a convincing explanation for the remarkable change in policy. In 1952 the possibilities inherent in the "new" or "people's democracy" had by no means been exhausted.

Humboldt University.
One day in the autumn of 1952 an old friend who had been my class-
mate in Berlin 1931-3 rang me up. Horst Krüger had been taken prisoner on the eastern front during the war and sent to a political training
course (*Antifaschule*) by the Soviet army. He returned to Berlin a convinced antifascist, completed his training in history and was now senior assistant in the Department of History at the Humboldt University.
The head of the department, Professor Schilfert, had instructed him to
make me an offer: if I would hold the course of lectures on general
history covering the period 1871 – 1914 the university would grant me
a three-year stipend for PhD candidates. Apparently this was Krüger's
idea, as Schilfert had not known me previously. Krüger knew that I was
acquainted with the history of Britain and international relations in the
period mentioned.
Although the proposed stipend plus lectures fees would mean a considerable reduction of my modest income, the offer was attractive. I was
losing interest in searching for exhibits and saw little chance of intellec-
tually demanding, creative work at the museum, where my suggestions were now usually rejected.
At the university there would be an opportunity of mastering a difficult task and of working with younger people. And if my lectures were
a success there might well be prospects of being appointed university
lecturer some time later. Meusel had no objections and therefore I
began to lecture in January 1953.
That a young man without a PhD degree should be entrusted with an
important course of lectures for about sixty students at this famous university was of course unusual. It was the result not of my academic
attainments – as yet unproven – but of the great losses the university
had suffered as a result of Nazism and war. Many of its best scholars
had been dismissed after 1933 because of their "non-Aryan" descent;
some had left because of their democratic sympathies. Quite a number
of younger lecturers had been killed in the war. And after January 1946,
when the university had been re-opened by the Soviet military administration, a considerable number of staff members had not been re-
appointed because of their Nazi affiliations. Some vacancies were for
the time being filled with old, already retired scholars, who volun-
teered to help reconstruct the university on a democratic basis, but
many chairs remained unoccupied. They were only gradually filled
during the next few years by scholars from other universities or re-

search bodies, and by professors who had been "de-nazified" as merely nominal members of the Nazi party.

As for history, in 1946 the chairs for ancient, medieval, and East European history were occupied by recognised scholars of the older generation, the chair for modern history in the following year by the appointment of Alfred Meusel. But because his duties as director of the Museum of German History had taken up nearly all his time since 1952, the younger Gerhard Schilfert was appointed to succeed him in the chair and as director of the Institute of General History founded at this time parallel to institutes for German and East European history.

The Institute of General History had three departments when I entered it: one for modern, one for medieval, and one for ancient history. The first of these was staffed by Schilfert as head, two senior assistants and three junior assistants, attached to it were a few candidates for doctorates living on stipends. Schilfert, whose professional qualities were of a high order, was engaged in research on the English revolution of the seventeenth century and related subjects and gave the lectures on general history covering the period 1500-1789. The senior assistant Gerda Grothe, a pupil of Meusel's and brilliant specialist in French history, lectured on general history for 1789-1870, and it was now my task to lecture to third-year students on the period 1871-1914. Lectures on general history after 1914 were not offered till the 1960s.

These lectures were, theoretically, meant to cover the globe except for Germany and Eastern Europe. In practice they concentrated on Europe; such subjects as the American War of Independence or the liberation of Latin America were treated only cursorily. The two neighbouring institutes at the same time provided introductory lectures on German and Eastern European i.e. mainly Russian and Soviet history. After the third year students were expected to specialize in one of the three fields; the majority always opted for German history.

Every week I had to prepare and hold a lecture lasting two academic hours (90 minutes) and after my second term, a seminar of the same length on questions arising out of my lectures. This was very hard going indeed, seeing that I had almost no previously written manuscripts on the large number of subjects to be outlined and commented on, and that in the 1950s there was not much literature on these subjects based on a democratic approach similar to or identical with mine. Soviet historians had done excellent work on medieval and early modern European history, and on French history up till 1871, but their surveys of "general history" after that year were not of the same standard. They were often factually unreliable and tended to offer simplifying, schematic applications of Lenin's theory of imperialism. They toned down the imperialist character of Russian foreign and colonial policy before the first world war and exaggerated the influence of the Russian revolution of 1905 in Europe and Asia. The sole exception, which was a real help, was the Soviet "History of Diplomacy", vol. 2 (1872-1919), published in German translation in 1947. Marxist and other left-wing historians from western Europe and the United States had written valuable surveys and studies on the social history and the labour and socialist movement of their countries, which I of course utilised, without always accepting their interpretations. But over long distances I had to find my way almost alone, occasionally including polemics against historians such as William L. Langer or Hans Herzfeld.

After almost a year I was so overworked that I suffered a serious breakdown and had to interrupt lecturing for six months. Then I resumed work, revising my text repeatedly during the following years. One thing I missed was that there was no helpful criticism from older colleagues. None of them ever turned up at any of my lectures to see how I was getting on. There was, none too often, criticism from students. At a party meeting where, as one of many items on the agenda, students were called on by the chairman to give their opinion on lectures, a student said that occasionally my German grammar was not quite in order (which was probably true), and that I pronounced English names wrongly: the pronunciation he had learned at school was quite different (which was presumably true as far as the second part of his criticism was concerned). At no time was there any attempt to criticize my lectures for ideological or political reasons.

During preparation for the PhD I was expected to acquire a passive knowledge of Russian and attend lectures on Marxist philosophy. The instruction in Russian was useful but the examination in that language turned out to be hardly more than a farce, since those taking part were allowed to use dictionaries. The lectures on philosophy were first given by Wolfgang Harich, later by Kurt Hager. The first was so brilliant that hundreds crowded into the largest lecture hall the university had at that time to hear him; the second was competent and respected. Later their paths diverged sharply: Harich landed in jail for conspiracy against the state, Hager rose to be Secretary of the Central Committee and member of the Politburo. Since their lectures offered me almost nothing I did not know already I attended only occasionally.

It was due to the friendliness, patience, and moral support of my first students that I resumed teaching in 1954 and survived as a lecturer.

With his students in Dresden, December 1955.

This class was more mature than later ones. All of them had experienced the war, about half of the men as young soldiers. Most were members of the SED by conviction; as far as I remember none of them had joined the party to gain admission to the university more easily. (In later classes this sort of dishonesty sometimes became apparent. Not that membership was a free pass to admission, but it could be an argument in favour of an applicant.) They knew what they wanted, worked hard, and did not avoid putting "awkward" questions, as later generations of students habitually tended to do.

My colleagues in the department were a friendly crowd. Most of them respected one another, but in my first years there were one or two cases in which respect turned out to be undeserved. A newly appointed professor of medieval history, for example, surreptitiously made use of German translations which he kept hidden on his lap under the table he was sitting at during seminars on medieval Latin texts. When his students discovered this one day he was, of course, discredited and soon after left for the Federal Republic. There he tried to gain favour by publishing a list of historians working in the GDR. But this man was an exception. As I repeatedly found when cooperating with members of our teaching staff, and as can easily be seen in their publications, the high reputations of Eduard Winter, Gerhard Schilfert, Joachim Streisand, Eckhard Müller-Mertens and others were well founded. All of us worked intensively, together with historians of other GDR universities, with the aim of creating a new panorama of German and world history basically different from the traditional German nationalist, imperialist and colonialist version once again being cultivated in the Federal Republic.

The 17th of June 1953.

On the morning of 17 June 1953 I went to the university as usual by city train from Lichtenberg station at about 8.40 a.m. At the station there were fewer travellers than usual and during the trip I could not help noticing that the streets looked empty. Only once a crowd was to be seen moving along a road. Friedrichstrasse station was also virtually empty; as I left it shortly after nine o'clock a railwayman closed the exit. People leaving with me said that our train had apparently been the last for the time being.

I wondered what was going on and walked to the university, which I entered from the rear. In the main building there were, it seemed, about twenty men, most of them party members and students belonging to the Free German Youth, determined to prevent any attempts by the crowd on the avenue Unter den Linden on the front of the building to intrude into it. The only member of our institute among them was Horst Krüger who told me that strikes had broken out and that traffic had stopped. Therefore only a few of those staff members and employees who normally would have turned up for work had been able to come – none of us had cars yet. Some may have preferred to stay at home. Since lectures had ended in the previous week not many students were obliged to be present.

In order to help if possible, I went down into the front court of the building, where some of our people were just locking up the gate securely. In Unter den Linden beyond the court a large crowd was moving to and fro excitedly in absolute disorder. Some people were shouting slogans such as "Down with Ulbricht" or "Away with the pointed beard", which also meant Ulbricht. A young man in baker's dress ran around waving the black, red and gold flag of the Federal Republic. Stones were thrown through the windows of the university and then a few men attempted to climb over the fence into the front court. They were driven back. Many people on the avenue had obviously come from West Berlin; their clothes were of a better quality than those we were accustomed to in the East of the city.

Gradually the people in the avenue ceased moving and fell loosely into groups, talking about what they should demand. At this stage the court gate was opened for a moment to let three of us out. I joined one of the groups, where a small, elderly man was just shouting "I want my business back. It's my property! I've got a right to it!" When I said to him "If you were a Nazi it was only just that you lost your business!" he took no notice. Other people standing there declared that rule by the SED should be ended, others said nothing but simply watched and listened. There was no real discussion; my impression was that people were just letting off steam. After moving about in the hullaballoo for some time I returned to the gate and was let in.

After my return a car drove slowly along Unter den Linden. A man sitting in it with a loudspeaker appealed for "law and order" and called on people to go home. The crowds began to disperse and the avenue was almost empty when a Soviet tank appeared and drove fast. From someone or other we heard that the Soviet army had taken over and a state of emergency had been proclaimed. Hours of silence followed. At 2 p.m. the city railways was still not operating and therefore, being no longer needed, I went off home on foot. Via Alexanderplatz and Frankfurter Allee I walked to Lichtenberg accompanied by one of the young assistants of our institute, who had joined us. During our walk of about two hours we saw Soviet troops at two places, but not many other people were in the streets which gave an impression of peace and calm. The assistant at my side was a Jew born in Berlin who had served in the British army in the war and taken part in the campaign to liberate Ethiopia from the Italians. He did not belong to the SED. Deeply upset by the events of the day, he told me that he had lost all confidence in the future of a democratic and non-racist Germany. I tried to clam him, pointing out that we had as yet not clear picture of what had happened, but to no avail. He left us for Israel shortly afterwards.

Of course I was upset too, because these events clearly showed that our leaders had made serious mistakes. One measure had been emphatically rejected by us shortly before the 17th of June: by decree private traders, owners of private service shops vital for the population such as hairdressers, shoe-makers, bakers, innkeepers as well as small manufacturers (who were very numerous) were – on May 1st! – to be deprived of their ration cards for meat and fats. It was an idiotic thing to do, because it condemned this large and important part of the population in the cities to living off the black market. The great difficulties in supplying the towns with food could not excuse an attack on these social groups or their indiscriminate classification as "capitalist elements". And why had the government raised production demands on industrial workers by at least 10 per cent? And abolished cheap return tickets for workers? These and other measures could even lead one to suspect that the idea had been to provoke unrest.

Recent research has shown that, apparently, decisions and "recommendations" of the Central Committee of the Communist Party of the Soviet Union were the reason for these provocative steps. It seems that Stalin's maleficent theory of the increasing severity of the class struggle in socialist countries had led to the notion that "capitalist elements" in the GDR society were "inevitably" an increasing danger to socialism in the making. Lenin's ideas on the necessity of cooperation with capitalists had been ignored. Of still greater importance for GDR policy in the first half of 1953 had evidently been Stalin's fear – not baseless but nonetheless exaggerated – of an aggression by the United States and its allies. It should, however, be added that the Soviet side recognised the course pursued in the GDR shortly before the 17th of June as wrong.

Why had our leaders – eight years after the war! – not known that such an outburst was coming? And not prepared the party for it? This was an inexcusable political defeat, no matter who had been responsible for the events, and it was only natural that there were many calls in the party for the dismissal of Ulbricht as General Secretary. After a heated dispute in the Central Committee he was nearly replaced by the editor-in-chief of the leading party newspaper, Rudolf Herrnstadt. My mother and I and, as far as I remember, all party members whom we knew, would have supported Ulbricht's re-moval.

But what had really happened? In some parts of the GDR nothing had happened at all, as in the cities of Chemnitz and Erfurt. Nearly all of Mecklenburg had remained quiet. Strikes took places mainly in Berlin and its surroundings, the industrial area of Sachsen-Anhalt (Magdeburg, Halle, Merseburg etc.) and the industrial towns of Jena and Gera. According to later findings rather less 10 per cent of the workers in the GDR had taken part. In some places SED and trade union organisers in the factories had prevented strikes by word-of-mouth propaganda.

Ulbricht characterized the events of the 17th of June as a "fascist putsch" and in the GDR this remained the official version for a long time. It is clear that Nazi elements saw their chance in the widespread discontent and play some part. In Halle, for example, a woman who had been an SS-guard at a concentration camp and was serving a life sentence in the city prison was set free by a mob and taken to the market place, where she made a wild speech to a crowd assembled there. The initiative for the strikes had come from Berlin building workers, who may well have been influenced by Nazis. After 1945 many former low-ranking officials and employees of Nazi institutions and organisations had been compelled by the new administrations to work as labourers in the building industry. (When helping to clear up ruins in Leipzig in 1949-50 I had noticed more than once that these people were influencing other building workers.)

But there had been no attempts to seize power anywhere and so no sign of an organisation directing the strikes and meetings. The demands raised were that the former production norms be restored, for better living conditions, for removal of Ulbricht and the government, and in some places for free elections. The term "putsch" was therefore out of place; it was an uncoordinated protest which may well have been surreptitiously triggered off by Nazis or by agents of the CIA. We will not know until the records of the US and Soviet security and espionage agencies have become accessible to historians.

One fact is indisputable: the powerful, US-controlled broadcasting station RIAS played an important, perhaps decisive part in inciting strikes and demonstrations from the afternoon of 16th June onwards. Between 5.30 and 7.30 a.m. on the following morning it broadcast three times a speech by the chairman of the West Berlin trade unions, Scharnowski (SPD), in which he called on his listeners to support a general strike in the GDR.

In the Federal Republic the events of the 17th of June were immediately called "a workers' insurrection" and this designation has remained customary in its literature. But there was, I repeat, no insurrection, no attempt to seize power by force or by peaceful means. There were strikes in quite a number of places for one or two days and the great majority of those who took part were of course workers. But how was it possible that workers went on the street against a government led by a party with deep roots in the industrial working class? A party whose members at this time were largely (about 40 per cent) workers themselves?

It was possible, first, because a high proportion of those employed as workers in industry, transport etc. were not of working-class origin but came from the lower middle class or the peasantry. Millions of Germans with such a social background had lost everything they possessed because of their expulsion from the territories ceded to Poland, from Czechoslovakia, Hungary and other countries, or by air attacks within Germany, or had lost their positions as clerks, salesmen, managers, policemen, teachers or professional soldiers. They had often been compelled, if they settled or lived in the Soviet Zone or later GDR, to seek employment as unskilled or semi-skilled workers. In many industries the workforce consisted to a high degree of people of this type. How high the degree was in 1953 will presumably never be known, but it was undoubtedly considerable, especially in industries employing much unskilled labour.

Second it was possible because several hundred thousand workers of proletarian origin, most of them members of the SED, had left the factories, mines, railways, postal services etc. to become policemen, "new teachers" trained in emergency courses, government employees of all grades and types, or to study at technical colleges or universities. Therefore the proportion of workers with a clear socialist orientation employed "at the work bench", so to speak, had decreased considerably. Under these circumstances the call for strikes and demonstrations against the government had clearly met less opposition than would otherwise have been the case.

In July a conference of the Central Committee of the SED approved a report by Ulbricht in which he attempted to analyse the mistakes made by the party leaders and the government. Although his analysis was hardly exhaustive he did admit that one cause of the mass protest was the thoughtless imitation of Soviet methods and practices. The shocking experience of 17th June 1953 drove the SED leadership and the administration on all levels to greater realism in day-to-day politics.

At the end of the year the supply of food and consumer goods was no longer as bad as it had been, but it still could not nearly satisfy the needs and wishes of the population. Conspicuous gaps remained in the supply situation throughout the 1950s, but on the whole it continue to improve.

Historical Science and Politics.
Historical teaching and research in the GDR from the very beginning developed in strict opposition to traditional, conservative German academic historiography of modern times, which since Leopold von Ranke and Heinrich von Treitschke had not only rejected the revolutions of 1789 and 1848 but had served the purposes of Prussian unification of Germany and later Germany's striving for world power. Academic historiography in the Weimar Republic had not broken with the powerful anti-democratic tradition of imperial Germany. On the contrary, many historians after 1918 had regarded the refutation of the "war guilt lie", with which the Allies had attempted to justify the Treaty of Versailles, as their most important task. Instead of searching for and uncovering the root causes of the First World War, hundreds of them

engaged themselves in attempts to prove that Germany was innocent or at least no more guilty than the Allies themselves. At the same time the glorification of Frederick II of Prussia and Bismarck continued unabated. The Republic gave more scope to liberal historians but not a single democrat, let alone socialist, was appointed to a chair of modern history. The Nazi regime was therefore easily able to accept the teaching staff for modern history at German universities except for a few professors of "non-Aryan" descent.

After 1945 helplessness and despondency among historians were overcome within a few years. But there was no democratic new start in German historical teaching and writing in the newly founded Federal Republic. As in other fields, the "experienced specialists" of former times were reinstated, with the exception of a handful of fanatical Nazis. Under Adenauer's reign variations of conservative nationalism dominated in the chairs for modern history.

Frederick II remained "the Great" and Bismarck, whose annexation of Alsace-Lorraine had made a further Franco-German war inevitable, remained "the architect of European peace". There was no attempt to seriously re-examine the origins of the First World War, and Hitler was often explained as "an historical accident".

The only new element, since about 1950, was the attempt to place Germany more in the context of European or "occidental" history. The leading conservative historian of the 1950s, Gerhard Ritter, turned "Luther the German" into a hero of the "Occident". This marked tendency was closely related to Adenauer's policy of an alliance with the Western powers. The inclusion of the Federal Republic in NATO evidently demanded history textbooks from each treaty power which did not deviate too much from each other and stressed the idea of a common European past. For this reason the Council of Europe organised six conferences from 1953 to 1958, at which historians and schoolteachers from all fifteen partners tried to arrive at versions which did not injure the susceptibilities of any of them.

Needless to say historical writing in the Federal Republic was anti-socialist, anti-communist and anti-Soviet. The historians of the GDR were often treated with resentful enmity, which I experienced when participating in a conference of the German Historical Association at Ulm in South Germany in 1956, in the company of about fifty of my colleagues. Following the example of leading historians like Gerhard Ritter and Hans Rothfels, most speakers from the Federal Republic simply ignored the contributions from our side. But many of the younger historians listened attentively to the indefatigable Alfred Meusel and other speakers from the GDR; those who had taken part in the previous conference of this association found that the atmosphere had improved (the 20th Congress of the Communist Party of the Soviet Union early in the same year may well have been one of the reasons). Soon after this, an association of historians of the GDR was founded.

The years 1956-60 were filled with hard work and important events in my private life. In 1957 I married and moved to my wife's home in Kleinmachnow near Potsdam, a very pleasant and quiet residential area on the south western border of West Berlin. Erika was a student and, when I came to know her, an energetic secretary of the Free German Youth branch at the history department. Her parents had an unusual background: they both came from German upper middle class families which had been resident for generations in St. Petersburg before the October Revolution. Her father had served in a guards' regiment of the Tsarist army as a second lieutenant towards the end of the First World War; after the Revolution they had both emigrated to Germany with their entire families. While most members of these families renounced all connections with Russia and became naturalised Germans, her parents had remained stateless and bilingual. They had, to the indignation of their relatives, joined the KPD in 1945, and her father had worked for the Soviet Military Administration as a translator. They had raised their three daughters in a spirit of allegiance to the GDR and friendship with the Soviet Union.

Six months after our wedding I was appointed university lecturer. Our first son was born in 1959; three years later a second followed. In 1960 we moved from my mother-in-law's house, in which we had lived after our marriage, to a small house nearby with a garden, right on the border. To reach the university we had to travel by city railway for an hour right through West Berlin.

Besides teaching I continued to work on my thesis on "The political relations between Germany and China 1861-1885", researched on the basis of the records of the German legation in Peking, which had survived two world wars and the Chinese revolutions in a Peking attic and had been handed over to the government of the GDR in 1950. These records enabled me to describe how the German minister – a picture book Prussian firebrand – had for the purpose of promoting "German interests" in China missed no opportunity of egging on his colleagues of the diplomatic corps to go ahead with the step-by-step subjection of the "Middle Kingdom" and its reduction to a joint semi-colony of the powers. The subject had been touched by Victor Kiernan in his book on *"Britain in China 1880 – 1885"*, but never dealt with in

At the international symposium on „One hundred years of African-German relations
1884-1984: the case of Cameroon" in Jaunde, April 1985. Second row from left to right:
Wolfgang J. Mommsen (London), Amadou Booker Sadji (Dakar),
M. Mohammed Mbodji (Dakar), Leonhard Harding (Hamburg), Helmuth Stoecker.
Third row, second from left: Buluda Itandala (Dar es Salam). Fourth row, first from left:
Ralph A. Austen (Chicago), second from left: Helmut Bley (Hanover).

detail before. The thesis was accepted by the Humboldt University.
After extending my account until 1894, I published it as a book. As a
pioneer study it was well received internationally, George Hallgarten
praising it in the *American Historical Review*. The only unfriendly re-
views came from West Germany.

At the same time there was criticism in a quarter from which I had not
expected it. The editor of the GDR *Zeitschrift für Geschichtswissenschaft*
in a long review accused me of "factology" – a term I had never heard
of and could not find in any dictionary. Perhaps he had invented it
himself. It was one of the very few words I encountered in the GDR
which faintly reminded me of George Orwell's 'Newspeak'. He meant
that I simply offered a factual account, without dealing with such theoretical (or political) aspects or conclusions as my results might offer,
which from his point of view was my duty as a Marxist. In my opinion this was not necessarily the duty of a Marxist historian at all.

My narrative had been written to put the record straight; it had no new
theoretical insights to offer and had never been intended to. At a meet-

In Jaunde, April 1985, at the rector's reception. From left: Yalla Eballa (Jaunde), H. Stoecker, W.J. Mommsen.

ing of the members of the institute the matter was discussed. No one supported the criticism, which was decisively rejected. Three of us wrote a reply and sent it to the journal, after it had been approved at a further meeting. But the editor, with whom I had collided once before at a party meeting, did not print it. Since the term "factology" was, to my knowledge, not used again in the journal or elsewhere, we left it at that.

The incident had no consequences except, presumably, one: to convince some readers that "factology" was a bad thing and that it was advisable to decorate one's own work with quotations from Marx, Lenin or other authorities, or with references to their writings. Usually such references were harmless since they did not lessen or increase the quality of whatever was presented.

My critic was a capable historian and later gained a reputation as an authority on the history of the German labour movement. He was not animated by the wish to advance his career by ferreting out and attacking deviations from a Marxist-Leninist "line". He was – of this I am certain – by nature intolerant and suspicious, and convinced that it was his duty to point out what he regarded as weaknesses in our work. Among the records handed over to the GDR by the Soviet Union at this time were those of the Imperial Colonial Office. There was also no lack of sources on German colonial affairs in the records of other government departments in the Central State Archive in Potsdam. Since I had long been interested in German colonial history, I began teaching it in seminars and suggested to a number of students that they write seminar papers and later MA theses on the basis of these records. By concentrating on Cameroon under German rule, a substantial amount of research on this colony resulted, some of which I edited and published in two volumes of papers (1960, 1968). They were not welcomed in the Federal Republic, but were in Cameroon itself. Together with an excellent book on the foundation of German East Africa published by another pupil of Meusel's in 1959, these publications began a refutation of the apologetic historical writing on German colonies which was to set the tone for some time yet in the Federal Republic and has not disappeared to this day.

The crisis of 1956.
The year 1956 saw the 20th Congress of the Soviet Communist Party in February and the rising in Hungary in October, accompanied by a crisis in Poland. The changes initiated in the Soviet Union since Stalin's death were liked in the GDR. Nikita Khrushchev soon became quite popular. He presented himself as a human being, not as an omniscient half-god, and his opinion that wars could be avoided and that peaceful co-existence of East and West for a long time to come should be aimed at was gladly supported by everyone I knew, inside and outside the SED.

But this happened mainly after the 20th Congress. After 1953 it was generally understood that the new order of things in eastern Germany had come to stay. One result of the stabilisation of the GDR and its gradual progress was the growth of the SED: its membership increased from 1.3 million in September 1953 to 1.4 million in April 1954, and to 1.6 million in December 1961. It should be emphasised that membership was voluntary; no one was forced to join, then or later. The overwhelming majority of those who applied for membership had become convinced that the party's arguments were sound and were prepared to support it actively, knowing that more than the regular payment of dues would be demanded from them.

Conditions for joining had been made more difficult: every application had first to be discussed and approved by the party group of the applicant's place of work (or residence, if she or he was not working). It was then considered by the party committee elected by all members of the branch to which the group belonged. Finally it went to the district committee elected by the delegates who had themselves also been elected at a meeting of the branch. On each level an application could be rejected and sent back to the next lower level for reconsideration.

Not every applicant was accepted. Especially very young people sometimes applied because of a passing mood, or because of constant admonitions within their family or from their colleagues, without really being mature enough for such a serious decision. Our party branch received many applications from students, which were often rejected or deferred for that reason. These applicants were usually told to think it over, do some "social work" in the youth organisation or elsewhere, and apply again in one or two years, if they still wanted to. Applications from students who were known to have no great liking for work or to have behaved immorally towards the other sex usually did not get any further than a short and sharp discussion in the undergraduate party group.

The motives of a small minority were unprincipled. Occasionally people without any political convictions tried to become members because they expected to derive this or that advantage from belonging to the ruling party, such as preferred admission to institutions of higher learning or more rapid promotion in their sphere of service or place of work. "Careerism" was in those years a serious offence in the SED and membership applications from people suspected of it were often rejected. But not all party organisations were as strict in this respect as ours was and even at the university I sometimes encountered "comrades" whose association with the SED was more formal than real.

The posthumous deposition of Stalin as one of the four classical authorities of Marxism-Leninism and the confidential but widely known revelations by Khrushchev of the terrible crimes committed on Stalin's orders were a surprise and a much more serious shock for the SED than the events of the 17th of June 1953. Our party organisation in the department of history was informed about the revelations in a circumspect way by one of the numerous members of the staff of the Central Committee at a meeting called for this purpose. (Although Khrushchev's full report was not published in the GDR till 1990, the version published in West Germany in June 1956 was circulated clandestinely in the GDR in the following months). On Stalin's deposition as a "classic" in theoretical matters he said that the works of the Marxist classical authors should not be treated as holy scripture.

Such an admonition should have been directed at the Party High School of the SED, whose director Hanna Wolf was (and remained) a dogmatist and worshipper of Stalin, and not at historians of Humboldt

University. Not only was there no one among us who regarded the works of Marx, Engels and Lenin as "revealed truth", but the director of the Institute of German history, Erich Paterna, had left the Party High School in 1953 because he rejected its dogmatic approach.

Not a few of us were accustomed to telling the students that the writings of Marx, Engels and Lenin contained analyses and reflections of genius as well as innumerable penetrating insights, but that they also sometimes erred and that on some matters their views, correct for their own times, were not, or not fully, valid for ours. And that the published texts the students were using could not, especially before the new collected works edition (MEW) was published (1956-90), be regarded as absolutely reliable. An example being the many articles by Marx published by the New York Daily Tribune of which no one could say where and how they had been altered or cut down by the editors. When – as happened occasionally in the 1950s and 1960s – students in a seminar paper attempted to prove the point they were making by quoting Marx or Engels as unimpeachable authorities they were given short shrift in my seminars, being told decisively that they had proved nothing.

Of course we agreed with the speaker from the Central Committee, but most of us saw no reason to re-interpret history in the light of the resolutions of the 20th Congress. Only the few who taught Soviet history felt it necessary to reconsider some points. They had been in the unenviable position of having had, more or less, to go along with Soviet assessments for the half-century after 1883, which were based on the "Short Course" of 1938. But even now they were unable to give a complete and truthful description of Soviet policies under Stalin, because the full truth was still kept secret. However, the lecturer who spoke on the October Revolution and the following years ventured to base his account largely on the publications of Trotsky, without naming his sources. Nobody objected. The work of the director of the institute, that splendid historian Eduard Winter, who belonged to no party and would not have claimed to be a Marxist, was not affected, since he neither wrote nor lectured on the history of the twentieth century.

In our institute there were some discussions on the results of the Congress, but our conclusions were gradual rather than immediate. Soviet historical science, until then regarded as authoritative, lost some of its reputation in our eyes, since parts of it had been burdened with distortions and falsifications due to Stalin and the entire system of the "personality cult" as Khrushchev inadequately called Stalin's dictatorship. There was more criticism on our side of nationalist tendencies in

Soviet historical literature, especially of the habitual whitewashing of the expansionist and colonial policies of Tsarist Russia.

Among GDR historians these tendencies had always been rejected. Meusel, for instance, in my presence in about 1953 scornfully quoted a school-book published in Moscow, in which the first partition of Poland (1772) was described thus: "Prussia robbed one part of Poland, Austria took another, and Russia received the third". In conversations with visiting Soviet historians we often cautiously broached the subject, only to find that their opinions varied widely. A.S. Yerussalimsky, who was a very good friend of ours and helped us a great deal, categorically rejected Russian nationalism and made no bones about the differences with his colleague A. L. Narotchnitsky on Russian expansion in Siberia.

It was now possible to criticise Soviet publications quite openly. For example Werner Müller and I published an extensive review of the German translation of a history of international relations in the Far East, in which we took the book's authors and the editors of that book to task for many errors and faulty interpretations, such as the exaggerated assessment of the echo of the Russian Revolution of 1905-7 in Asia.

On the whole one can say that, in spite of an ideological tightening-up in the SED after the Hungarian counter-revolution and the end of the "thaw" in the Soviet Union, the 20th Congress of the Soviet Communist Party resulted in the GDR in more open discussion and greater readiness to put forward new ideas among scholars.

More shocking and painful than the deposition of Stalin as an authority on Marxist theory were the revelations about the crimes committed on his orders or at least with his approval. Even if we assumed that the official saga about Trotskyism and about Bukharin, Zinoviev, Kamenev and others was largely true, these crimes upset not a few among us deeply and posed puzzles which were to be finally solved only many years later. After the congress Khrushchev had said that whatever Stalin might have done, he had always acted in the belief that he was serving socialism. That might be true – many acts of Stalin, not least towards Germany, supported such a view – but it explained nothing. Khrushchev's explanation had been the fundamentally wrong and un-Marxist "cult of personality". Did such a cult, which the German socialist movement had known in connexion with Ferdinand Lassalle (1825-1864), mean that the first socialist power on earth, which had played a decisive role in the defeat of fascism, could sink to the level of oriental despotism of centuries long past?

Obviously Russia's backwardness in many spheres and the complete lack of democratic traditions outside the working class movement were important parts of any explanation. But, since there was almost a clamp-down on the whole subject in Moscow after 1956, the question remained open and continued to perplex and worry many of us.

At an excited meeting of undergraduate SED members a few months after the Congress, at which various points of view were put forward, I said that the Communist Party of the Soviet Union was the oldest and strongest communist party on earth, that it had a long and heroic past, and that the GDR would not be able to exist without its support. The Soviet Communist Party had not been spared tragic errors and grievous miscarriages of justice, but we should never forget how much we and mankind as a whole owed to this party and the Soviet Union. At the time, considering how little we knew, it was hardly possible to say more. But I did not feel happy about my statement and was well aware that it could not satisfy the critical spirits I had spoken to. What my fellow party members and I did not know was the magnitude and true character of Stalin's evil, barbaric legacy, which had injured and compromised the socialist cause to such an appalling extent.

As a sequel to the 20th Congress discussions began in our party organisation on the need for more democracy in the party and the republic. A very vocal student even founded a "Jacobin Club" which met regularly at a restaurant near the university to exchange ideas. Less radical but radical enough to draw an emphatic rejection from the university party committee, were the views of the party secretary of the department, a young lecturer in medieval history. At heated meetings of the department party committee, to which I belonged at the time, two historians from the Institute of Marxism-Leninism, specially delegated for the purpose, attempted to convince the secretary and the more numerous part undecided committee members that his views were erroneous. But he did not give way. Finally he was deposed as secretary by the university committee and replaced by a younger member of the department who toed the party line. Disappointed, the former secretary buried himself in his professional work and became one of the best-known medieval historians of the GDR.

When the political crisis in Poland in October 1956 found an end with the election of Wladislaw Gomulka as party leader, the East Berlin evening newspaper printed the full text of his inaugural speech. In it Gomulka promised greater democracy for his people, and for this reason the Central Committee of the SED disapproved of the publication, and prevented the distribution of the newspaper at the last minute.

This act was strongly resented by two of my colleagues and me, who met in the institute on the following morning. We pinned a protest on the notice board, thereby drawing upon us the wrath of the university party secretary Hans Singer (a refugee in Switzerland during the war). He had the protest removed and instructed the party secretary of our department to criticise its authors severely for their "political blindness" in not seeing that the GDR was not Poland. This argument made me uncertain of my position, and I left the matter at that. Were democracy and free speech not necessary attributes of socialism? Of course they were! Lenin had said that every cook must learn to govern. But it was clear that under conditions of war this important tenet could not be fully put into practice; there must be limitations, even on freedom of speech, for those who supported socialism. And was the Cold War not a war? Evidently Ulbricht and other leaders feared that a general discussion on more democracy in the GDR might lead to unrest ending in a repetition of 17th June 1953. Were they right or were they wrong? The Hungarian counter-revolution seemed to show that they were right. (There can be no doubt that in Hungary the popular protest movement against an inept and stupid leadership had paved the way for a genuine counter-revolution which aimed at restoring capitalism.) And did not the aggression of Britain, France and Israel against Egypt and the Soviet Union's threat to intervene just at this time show that the Cold War could easily turn into a hot war?

To which extent and for how long were limitations on civil rights – except for fascists and criminals – compatible with the construction of socialism? Would not such limitations, if they lasted too long, by force of habit become a matter of course and impair the quality of life to such a degree that socialism would lose one of its essential qualities, democracy? And the peoples living in such socialist countries would turn against it. This cluster of problems weighed heavily and was to prey on my mind for many years to come. I spoke about it often with my mother and with close friends.

Our attitude towards the party leader Ulbricht was reserved. Wilhelm Pieck, who had virtually retired from the leadership in 1952 because of failing health, did not possess the intellectual abilities of Ulbricht, but his unassuming and natural way of dealing with people had brought him popularity and considerable authority. He was a genuine father-figure. The younger Ulbricht, on the other hand, was never popular, neither in the party nor with the population. His falsetto voice, coupled with a strong Saxon accent, were handicaps which in other parties would have precluded a political career. But he was a personality of great strength and a skilful tactician, obviously to be preferred by far to a well-meaning but inexperienced intellectual such as Wolfgang Harich, who was arrested in November 1956, one month after the counter-revolution had begun in Hungary, and sentenced to ten years' imprisonment for propagating far-reaching reforms and plotting to overthrow the Politburo.

The reforms he demanded were of such a nature that the GDR would hardly have survived them: a new leadership, a "specifically German road to socialism", changes in the relations with the Soviet Union.

Ulbricht owed his position as second in command of the German Communist Party in 1945 largely to the fact that he was one of the very few leaders of the party to have survived the Nazi regime and that he was trusted by the leaders of the Soviet and other parties. During the years 1928-45 he had spent most of his time in the Soviet Union and he undoubtedly regarded government by a highly centralised bureaucratic apparatus as natural and necessary for socialist states confronted with the unrelenting enmity of the capitalist great powers. After the 20th Congress in Moscow there was a widespread feeling in the SED that, whatever merits he might have, the leadership should be placed in other hands.

But who was to take his place? My mother and I, in common with some friends, thought of Karl Schirdewan, a member of the Politburo since July 1953. She had heard from some old acquaintances of hers who worked in the Central Committee that he held views different from those of Ulbricht on the conclusions to be drawn from the Congress, to emphasise the need to return to Lenin's principles more strongly and to take an active interest in the welfare of German communist victims of Stalin's persecutions who at this time were returning to Germany.

My mother had been horrified to discover such a case during a visit to relations in the Rhineland in 1957. She had met a woman named Helene Tidemann, whom she had known before the First World War. This woman had emigrated to the Soviet Union with her husband in 1932, where he was arrested five years later and sentenced to ten years in a camp in Siberia. She had never heard from him again and returned from Omsk, where she had been sent when war began, in 1955 ill and penniless. My mother wrote to Schirdewan about her, and he saw to it that she received aid.

But after the Hungarian counter-revolution he gradually lost his influence and was expelled from the Central Committee early in 1958. In an interview with him broadcast in 1991 the interviewer aptly described him as "a hesitant rebel". His opposition to Ulbricht had not been decided enough: it was evidently hamstrung by his conviction that he had to observe "party discipline". Ulbricht remained party leader till 1971. In accordance with Ulbricht's interpretation of "democratic centralism" (which was obviously different from that of the author of this principle of party life, Lenin) Schirdewan had never had the chance of putting his views to the party as a whole. But the SED survived the crisis of 1956 without outwardly recognisable losses. As for me, I suppose I had been "a hesitant critic", like many party members. For this there were many reasons.

The GDR in the late 1950s.
My wife and I felt on the whole quite happy in the first years after 1957. Things were going well for us and the GDR in general. We were healthy, as was our first boy, we had a small house of our own in a very quiet and pleasant quarter of Kleinmachnow, our neighbours were nice and helpful, our jobs were fascinating, and we had successes to boot: Erika passed her finals with distinction and could begin work on a doctoral thesis, and I, besides publishing my first books, presented a paper at a conference in East Berlin of historians from various countries on the Second World War, dealing with British and French policy in September 1939, which found so much favour that in the publication of the proceedings it was included twice!

The upward trend in the GDR in 1957-8 was unmistakable. Conditions improved in many ways. Industrial production rose perceptibly, and the rationing of meat, fats and sugar ended in 1958. Medical services, equally accessible to everyone on the basis of compulsory insurance, improved; the number of holiday homes maintained by the trade unions increased in leaps and bounds and put very cheap tourism in the most beautiful areas of the Republic within the reach of hundreds of thousands, later millions of workers and their families. In education more and more young people were making use of the chances which the disappearance of class privileges was offering them. The mood of people in general obviously improved; in the SED, with nearly one-and-a-half million members in 1957, there was increasing optimism that socialism would be achieved, in spite of recurring economic difficulties.

Optimism also resulted from the progress of colonial liberation. The last French troops had been forced to leave Vietnam in 1955 and the enduring struggle of the Algerian army of liberation in the following years broke the back of French colonialism in Africa. Britain had been forced to evacuate the Suez Canal in 1956; in 1957 it had conceded independence to Ghana. Two years later revolutionary forces under Fidel Castro gained power in Cuba. These and other defeats of the leading colonial powers became possible to a considerable extent because of the political support of the Soviet Union for many liberation movements. We regarded the world-wide overthrow of nearly the whole of the colonial system, I think justly, as an important advance for humanity. But when I learned of the enormous sums the Soviet Union was providing for the erection of the Aswan high dam I wondered if, in view of Egypt's uncertain political future, the money would not have been better invested in Soviet agriculture or consumer good industries. Probably these doubts were justified.

Erika and I visited the Soviet Union for the first time in 1958 with a GDR tourist group to have a look at Moscow, Kiev and Rostov. With her fluent Russian she was able to talk with many people of all walks of life during our three weeks' trip. We were not disappointed, quite the contrary. What impressed us most were the quiet dignity of the working people we encountered, their friendliness towards us GDR Germans, the conspicuous absence of advertisements in the streets and the tube, the absence of cheap trash in bookshops and newspaper kiosks, the magnificent flower-beds in the streets of Kiev and Rostov. What did not impress us were the state of public toilets, the general use of abacuses by saleswomen and cashiers in shops, and the employment of women as street cleaners. Only later, in the 1960s and 1970s, did we get some idea of the basic weaknesses and defects of the Soviet Union. There was some connection – I am still uncertain of its nature – between the upward movement in the GDR and new tones in party policy, which now influenced attitudes and behaviour in a very general way difficult to measure, but undoubtedly real. A concerted effort was made to popularise socialist morals, to encourage a "socialist way of life", and to combat prejudices and conduct associated with the petty bourgeoisie. In the cinemas a film was shown in which a popular actor, Herbert Köfer, played an old working-class communist who is party secretary in a medium-sized construction works. The technicians are a good crew and he gets on well with all of them. But one day, he accidentally discovers that one of these men, a talented young engineer, is building himself a weekend bungalow in a beautiful forest. The secretary is taken aback and disappointed.

At a meeting of the technicians he tells the young man in no uncertain terms that he is misled by petty bourgeois ideas of a good life. Why does he not spend his free time studying to raise his qualification, or playing in a football team for his works? His colleagues agree with the party secretary and the young engineer, ashamed of himself, promises to mend his ways. But is his promise honest?

The future will tell.

In 1958 the 5th Party Congress had decided on "Ten commandments of socialist morals and ethics", which besides direct political demands included the following:

"5. In building socialism you must act in a spirit of mutual help and loyal cooperation, respect the collective and take its criticism to heart ...

7. You must constantly seek to improve the results of your work, be economical and uphold labour discipline.

8. You must educate your children in the spirit of peace and socialism to become people of many-sided culture, of firm character and a sturdy physique.

9. You must live cleanly and decently and respect your family."

A year later, in a speech he held to introduce the Seven-Year Plan, Ulbricht spoke of "the socialist community of man", which was developing in the GDR, and in 1960 he described it in detail. This concept was put in a nutshell in the motto "Forward from me to us", meaning "Go ahead from egoism to collectivism". To underline that we were entering a new stage of social life, some new titles and ceremonies were introduced.

Teams of workers with successes to their credit were promoted to "brigades of socialist labour" and given a small bonus in addition to their normal pay. A similar status (or rather decoration) as "activist" was bestowed upon exceptionally good individual workers, who received a medal and a bonus of 300 or 400 marks which for many amounted to more than half a month's wages. Usually the trade union committee of a factory or department would decide who was to be decorated; later the assent of the party committee became essential.

The brigade members were encouraged to associate outside working hours. To raise their "culture standard" funds were made avaible to the brigades for joint visits to the theatre or light opera. (Since there was a tendency to spend this money in restaurants or public houses after the performances, its use had to be strictly accounted for later.) In East Berlin's best theatres, which we frequented at this time, one or two rows were regularly reserved for such brigades. Authors were engaged for readings in industrial plants, painters were invited to exhibit their pictures on factory premises, or commissioned to paint new pictures to be hung there. In theatres, cinemas and concert halls there was some (not nearly enough) light entertainment, but the low-level, cheap, commercialised kinds of films, plays or music for mass consumption to be found in all western countries were kept out.

To emphasise the socialist character of our society, a ceremony was revived which had a long tradition in the German working class movement: after completing eight years of school boys and girls were festively introduced into adult society with music, flowers and solemn speeches at a meeting in which their teachers, classmates, and family took part. The main speech at these *Jugendweihe* (youth initiations) was usually given by some person of standing or public figure, rather like speech day at British secondary schools, but here devoted to advise the youngsters on how to make a success of their lives in a socialist society. Two other ceremonies introduced at this time were entirely new: "socialist christenings" ("name-giving") of the new-born and "socialist weddings". The first I never witnessed but read and heard about.

It was organised by commissions set up by the communal authorities, consisting of members of organisations such as the women's league, of the parents' councils attached to schools etc., and took place about twice a year in the houses of culture each locality had, or the wedding room of the registry office. Parents would report their wish to take part beforehand and then attend with the new-born child and two or three godparents. There was a solemn ceremony, with a choir singing or a small orchestra playing chamber music, and a speech by some local bigwig, greeting the new members of the socialist community. There was no prescribed ritual. Usually these ceremonies were enacted for a number of children, whose names had of course been chosen by the parents and already entered at the registry office.

A "socialist wedding" I also never took part in; but it was described to me at the time in detail by a woman I knew. She had married a schoolteacher. Both were convinced socialists and among the first to be married in this way. The ceremony, like all "socialist weddings", was enacted at the place of work of one of the partners, in this case the hall in the school of her fiancé. The school choir sang, the headmaster made a speech, the registrar who had come to the school for the purpose declared the couple husband and wife, the couple exchanged rings, the choir sang again, everyone present offered congratulations. "Socialist christenings" and "socialist weddings " never became generally popular and both petered out around 1970.

The *Jugendweihe*, on the other hand, enjoyed much popularity and became a standing institution. Nearly all youngsters took part; only a small minority, whose parents regarded these ceremonies as incompatible with church confirmation, stayed away.

Some of these innovations were introduced in our university. Instead of "brigades" there were "collectives of socialist labour" who often spent their joint bonus on an excursion or visit to the theatre.

"Activists" were nominated in the same fashion as in industrial enterprises. The scholars thus favoured were usually just as satisfied about it as any worker or technician, although their chances of winning some higher state decoration, with a much higher financial premium attached, were far greater than for members of any other profession except for arts and letters.

Students were now to be encouraged to write their seminar essays and even examination papers and theses jointly, i.e. two or three of them submitted manuscripts as the result of "socialist cooperation" between them. I quickly put an end to such nonsense in my seminars, and my colleagues, finding that many papers of this kind were being written by one student while one or two weaker ones simply put their names to them, or that the contributions of the authors were obviously unequal but could not be measured singly, also stopped the practice.

There was an excited party meeting at which several students praised the virtues of "socialist cooperation". My turn came, and I said that mutual help among students, especially by the strong for the weak, should always be encouraged, and that every socialist student should feel responsible for the performance of her or his whole seminar group. But the weak should never be allowed to hide their weakness behind the strong. After leaving the university, all students would have to show what they were capable of individually and not as couples or groups. The dispute ended with a compromise: papers written by more than one student were to be accepted if the part each author had written was clearly distinguishable from other parts. In the upshot papers of this kind were not often written at our university; they became fairly common at the newly founded high schools maintained by the parties, the trade union federation etc.

A further innovation was the *Hausgemeinschaft* (house community), founded for the purpose of bringing town and city dwellers closer to each other in their places of residence. Since the majority of the population lived in towns and cities, usually as tenants of flats and not of family houses, these "communities" came to include many millions of people. To found a *Hausgemeinschaft* a tenant in a house comprising between four and twenty separate flats (often but by no means always an SED member) invited the other tenants to a talk in his flat. They discussed elementary matters concerning them all, such as the cleanliness of the staircase, repairs needed, noise and other disturbances, neighbourly help etc. Then they elected a chairman and a treasurer, and thus founded a body which was a legal entity entitled to agree contracts with the house owners. The latter would, if the tenants wished it, transfer a small sum of money every month as remuneration for cleaning the stairs and other jobs – since it was difficult to find people for this sort of work, they were usually glad if the tenants did it. The "house communities" would normally meet about once a month. They were an entirely voluntary affair. Their treasurers sometimes even collected the monthly rent.

When we moved into a very large house in Berlin in 1970 we found that the last of several attempts to constitute such a body there had just failed. There was one further meeting of the tenants about some pressing problems such as the refuse collection, which was unreliable, but most tenants were not interested and did not attend. In many houses with a large number of flats it was difficult to keep such a body going. When we moved into a smaller house in a quieter area in 1976 we joined a house community that had been going well for years. The tenants jointly kept the house clean, looked after the flowers on the stairs, carried out small repairs by themselves and even occasionally organised get-togethers with cake and coffee. Naturally not all tenants showed the same interest, but the institution was accepted by all as useful.

These and other attempts to promote the "socialist community of man" were not always shrewdly conceived or sufficiently prepared. Some were downright naive. But they would not have been possible without a background of economic progress – modest as it was – and the growing feeling that social barriers were fading away. A working class for whom universities had been a strange, inaccessible sphere could now send its children there. "The *Proleten* (proles) are governing" a middle-class woman had said to me disgustedly in 1949 – now, ten years later, the middle class people who had not moved West, were, in most cases, finding their places in the new society.

Some of them had become its active defenders. Among my mother-in-law's friends there was an elderly gentleman named Fritz Brauer, once member of an estate owning family in the province of Posen and a Prussian guards officer who had served on the staff of General Groener in the First World War. Later a forestry expert, he had joined the Christian Democratic Union in the Soviet Zone in 1945 and was elected to the People's Chamber for that party in 1950. When I came to know him in Kleinmachnow, he missed no opportunity to defend the GDR to all and sundry.

In the late 1950s arguments had become easier to find. For instance: although the Federal Republic was being built up again much more quickly and was nicer to look at, it had a much higher crime rate. Its central railway stations were notorious as haunts of all sorts of criminals. In the GDR, on the other hand, the crime rate had sunk more and more. Armed robbery was now almost extinct. According to official figures, there were in 1960 350 cases of robbery and extortion, and 89 cases of murder and manslaughter. The figures for the Federal Republic were, if population totals are taken into consideration, in the same year five times higher for robbery and double for murder and manslaughter. When my mother-in-law visited her elder sister in Wiesbaden in the Federal Republic, she was surprised about warnings not to enter certain areas of the town because they were unsafe. Such areas were unknown in the cities of the GDR. When that sister visited her in Kleinmachnow, she was surprised that people there did not lock up their gardens when they went out: there was no need to.

There was one feature of life in the GDR which seldom disappointed us, namely culture. Literature, the theatre, films and the fine arts were all heavily subsidised by the state, the funding coming from general revenue and, to a small extent, from a minimal surcharge on cinema and theatre tickets. A commercial approach was kept out of this sphere almost entirely during the whole duration of the GDR, which was surely no mean achievement.

German classical literature was published from the very beginning in large editions at very low prices, including of course Heine's works, which had been suppressed by the Nazi regime. The same preferential treatment was accorded to the works of famous authors persecuted by the Nazis, most of whom had been forced to emigrate, such as Heinrich Mann, Arnold Zweig, Anna Seghers, Bertolt Brecht, Lion Feuchtwanger, Leonhard Frank, and to self-taught working class writers associated with the communist movement like Willi Bredel, Jan Petersen and Hans Marchwitza. Translations of the novels and short stories of all great Russian writers from Pushkin to Gorky (expect, for a long time, Dostoyewsky) and of Soviet authors were to be found in all bookshops. The works of many authors of other nations were also published, not only left wingers like Louis Aragon, Sean O'Casey or Jorge Amado but also those such as George Bernard Shaw, Graham Greene and Carson McCullers, to mention only a few of a myriad.

What cheered us especially was the appearance of many new authors, children of the GDR so to speak. Some of these soon became popular: Erwin Strittmatter, Dieter Noll, Bernhard Seeger, Wolfgang Joho,

Helmut Sakowski. Barred on principle were German nationalist and Nazi writers. Hans Grimm, Ernst Jünger and the like were even excluded from communal lending libraries. Novelists from the Federal Republic hostile to the GDR were usually not published either, and the products of the best-seller author Konsalik, who depicted German soldiers of the Second World War as heroes, were even confiscated when found in travellers' luggage at the border.

There was one serious hindrance to publishing, especially in the early years: for quite a few works that GDR publishers wanted to print the copyright was held by publishers in the Federal Republic (or, in one case, in Sweden) who refused to give licenses or demanded fees which were considered too high. For such reasons the works of the greatest German author of our century, Thomas Mann, were not to be found in our bookshops for some time. Sometimes books published in the Federal Republic or Austria were sold in the GDR, but at prices too high for many who wanted to buy them. At other times licenses were given only for very small editions. These books usually disappeared under the counter and unless one's relations to the bookseller were very good the chances of getting a copy were slight.

Anyway, by the 1960s the GDR had become a *Leseland* (reading country). In 1967 20.4 per cent of the entire population were registered as readers in public and trade union libraries and nearly 20 million copies of books of the category *belles-lettres* were printed, more than a third of them translated from other languages.

In the 1950s and 1960s the leading theatres in East Berlin could claim to be the most interesting in the whole of Germany. Bertolt Brecht's *Berliner Ensemble* made its mark on world theatre history and Walter Felsenstein's *Komische Oper* revolutionised the whole concept of opera. Many of the best films the *DEFA* produced at its studios near Potsdam were based on novels by the authors mentioned above; they were seen and applauded by millions. Painting – expect for the significant Bert Heller, one of whose pictures hung in our department – lagged behind the other arts, but sculpture, represented by outstanding men like Fritz Cremer, Theo Balden and Heinrich Drake, reached a level to be proud of.

We eagerly enjoyed all this and felt confirmed in our conviction that the GDR, whatever faults it might have, was a worthwhile affair and the better of the two German states. Any assessment of the GDR which ignored its literature and arts would be jaundiced indeed.

The Wall.
Early in the morning of the 13th of August 1961 I was abruptly awakened by a messenger sent by the party secretary for Kleinmachnow (the only full-time party employee in the settlement) who informed me that the border was being closed and asked me to walk around in our neighbourhood with another member living close by until midday. Should we notice anything unusual we were to phone him immediately. Surprised, I gulped down some coffee and went to fetch my companion, an engineer whose job it was to organise the annual "fairs for the master technicians of tomorrow " in Leipzig. We walked around and noticed nothing whatever, except for a slanging match at the border control point between a small fat N.C.O. with two soldiers as the sole visible representatives of state authority and some youths who had obviously intended to go to West Berlin and were now unable to do so. This was obviously not the sort of thing we had been asked to report and we broke off our walk after a couple of hours.

During the following weeks the border, until then almost open, was closed by the erection of wire fencing. For the inhabitants of Kleinmachnow the results were serious. Those who had worked in West Berlin had to find jobs in the GDR, the many who were employed in East Berlin now had to travel to work by a route right around half of Berlin either in their cars or by bus, railway and then city rail, changing two or even three times. The tour by bus and train took at least one-and-a-half, sometimes two hours or more, since the newly established suburban railway service from East Berlin to Potsdam was neither fast nor reliable. Everybody soon ironically called the trains *Sputnik* – Yuri Gagarin's flight into space had taken place only a few months previously.

The university was on summer holiday in August and it was only weeks after the 13th that the staff members could consider the consequences. The two staff members of our department who lived in West Berlin said that they would remain in their positions. The authorities in their part of the city had decided to change part of the salaries of those West Berliners who worked in the East into West German money and therefore they would be able to carry on. But one of them, a lecturer, nonetheless left us shortly after. A very sensitive person, she had been shocked to witness how some people who had tried to pass the border illegally were handled. The loss for the institute was a serious one. Other parts of the university were badly hit, the department of physics, for instance, losting its three professors. But term began as usual in September.

After the Federal Republic joined the West European Defence Community the GDR had erected controls over traffic across its western borders, stiffened in 1952 by a prohibited zone five kilometres wide. But any citizen of the GDR could pass freely to West Berlin at any time and, equipped with a provisional passport obtained there, fly out to West Germany (and back again if he or she wished). Some people we came to know in the rocky hills of Saxony had, as they confidentially told us, gone to Austria for a holiday the year before by this route.

"The Wall", provisionally erected piece by piece during the following years between the two parts of Berlin, was therefore at first regarded by a considerable part of the population of East Berlin, the area surrounding the former German capital, and to a lesser extent the rest of the GDR, with indignation and dejection. No wonder: many, especially elderly people who had during their whole life been accustomed to visiting friends and relations in what had become "the other Germany" were now limited to communication by phone and letter. It was no longer possible to buy quality goods in West Berlin (at prices inflated by an exchange rate for the two currencies harmful for the GDR economy). And it was no longer possible to leave the GDR for good, or temporarily for private visits to the Federal Republic or Western countries without the permission of the GDR authorities which was rarely given except for pensioners (after 1964). But on the whole people accepted "the Wall" passively. While travelling home one day I heard a man good-humouredly saying to another who wore a party badge: "Well, you can do what you like with us now."

In the SED and among the many outside its ranks who supported the socialist cause, on the other hand, there was a feeling of assent (I heard of a woman who broke out into tears of happiness on learning that "world peace had been saved"), of relief at the end of a situation that had obviously become untenable, or of cautious reserve because of fear of what the results might be. How much attitudes varied among people in general showed itself in my wife's family a few days after the closing of the border: one of her cousins, a young woman being trained for work in the Protestant church, visited Erika's younger sister, a hospital nurse. The cousin on entering the house could not contain her feelings and exclaimed: "My god! Isn't it terrible! " My sister-in-law, at that time undecided about the GDR, replied with no less passion: "But this is the best thing that happened for years! It was high time that

Ulbricht let the shutters down!" The cousin, after recovering from this reply, changed the subject.

The reasons for this drastic step were complex. As "Front Line City" West Berlin had since 1949 been a very serious thorn in the flesh of the GDR, economically and politically. There is no doubt that economic advance had been badly hampered by illicit trading over the open border and the constant drain on manpower by the exodus of young people enticed away by the higher standard of living in the Federal Republic (Never, after all, had a state passively accepted a mass exodus of parts of its population if the welfare of those remaining at home was endangered.) Bad blunders in economic policy worsened the situation, which was approaching a general crisis in summer 1960. The economic aims of the 5th Party Congress of 1958 and the Seven Year Plan for 1959-65 had proved to be too ambitious; the "main economic aim" of overtaking the Federal Republic in average consumption figures had turned out to be illusory. The overrapid foundation of farming cooperatives plunged agriculture into such difficulties that a kind of unofficial rationing of meat and butter had to be introduced for some time. In Kleinmachnow the supply of food, textiles and many other goods in the shops became worse. At the same time the number of people who took employment in West Berlin increased noticeably. Among them was one of our neighbours, a worker living in the upper part of the house next door. The traffic policeman who occupied the lower part, an SED member, told him off so vigorously a few weeks before the 13th of August that he returned to his job in a factory near Kleinmachnow.

The lack of realism in economic leadership had been evidently to some degree due to what was later politely called the subjectivity of Khrushchev, who in his desperate search for remedies for the perennially catastrophic state of Soviet agriculture had fallen victim to charlatans and preached the cultivation of maize as a plant that would improve farming results beyond all measure. This idea was rejected by agricultural scientists in the GDR, but the SED seriously attempted to push forward the planting of maize on 10 per cent of the arable land of the republic. In press propaganda it was called the "sausage on a bough" and of course it had its uses, but our farmers knew better than to regard it as a panacea for their difficulties. I heard that the figures they reported on maize cultivation to the administration were often exaggerated. A more serious mistake had been the large-scale introduction of open-air cow-sheds, for which our climate was unsuitable. In the winter months milk returns sank steeply and cattle mortality rose.

I did not witness developments in agriculture or industry, but knew quite a number of people who did. From news from a friend of my mother's who was secretary of the association for mutual aid among peasants in Thuringia, from conversations with Siegbert Kahn who received much unpublished information on economic matters, from the remarks of colleagues doing "party work" in Berlin electrical works and from many other sources I was able to see fairly clearly what was happening. There was much discussion about our economy, especially after the preparations for the production of aeroplanes in Dresden had been broken off in March 1961, with losses amounting to billions of marks. It seems that the decision was due to changes in the Soviet aircraft industry after the invention of intercontinental rockets. The sudden end to this project disappointed many young people.

At the same time the Cold War threatened to escalate into an atomic war – this fact, pushed into the foreground by Ulbricht in his defence of the closing of the border, was obvious. But the Wall, assented to by all Warsaw Pact governments on the 3rd to the 5th of August 1961, did not "save the peace". It helped the GDR to master its difficulties. Ulbricht's term for the Wall, "antifascist protective rampart" – which was the official designation for many years to come –, was hardly appropriate, since the Federal Republic, while no shining example of democracy, was certainly not fascist.

Opinions on the motives for the building of the Wall are highly controversial. It seems clear, however, that it was at first not intended to be a long-term solution. Its erection slightly behind the east-west border in Berlin began in October and in its provisional form it was completed in 1964.

The imposition of a strict control on the borders with West Berlin could hardly be avoided under the circumstances. By no means necessary was the manner in which it was done. Scarcely any walls to protect towns, or parts of towns, had been built in Europe since the sixteenth century (except around Jewish ghettos), and it should have been clear that the Berlin Wall would be a gift to anti-communist propaganda the world over. A broad and deep ditch flanked by wire fencing would have fulfilled the purpose of a barrier just as well and could not have become such an optically effective symbol. Here, and not only here, the leaders of the GDR showed a psychological insensitivity difficult to believe.

Of still greater importance for the GDR in the 1960s was the introduction of a border regime which amounted, for the time being, to a complete end of private traffic between West Berlin and the GDR. This did not only mean a stop to the illicit export of millions of marks in GDR currency every month to West Berlin, which had meant constant losses for the GDR economy, but also an end to the purchase of goods and services (for instance hairdressing, automobile repairs, photo developing) by West Berliners which were much cheaper in East than in West Berlin. It also meant an end to the employment of GDR citizens in West Berlin, according to some reports the total was about 30,000. These were important economic gains, but the political price need not have been so high. Private visits from both sides could well have been permitted much sooner and to a far greater extent than was done from August 1961 until September 1964 and afterwards.

Our life in the 1960s.

After the excitement of the first weeks after the 13th of August 1961 had subsided, years of calm economic progress for the GDR set in, marked by increasing internal stability and advances in many spheres of life. But some of the advances produced new contradictions and difficulties, which might have been avoided or overcome if the political system had now begun to scale down its undemocratic features. On the whole it can be said that economic successes were notable but that there was no political or ideological advance to match it; at any rate not to such a degree that wholesale progress "on all fronts" could be carried over into the 1970s and surmount the gigantic obstacles to come. The symptoms of democratic underdevelopment (to put it mildly), became more obvious after Khrushchev had been succeeded by Brezhnev, a man of less vision and with no popularity in the GDR.

Neither my family, nor my colleagues, nor I myself fully understood at the time what was happening in our republic. While the newspapers and other media reported not without bias but seriously and comprehensively on events in the capitalist world, it was impossible to gain a realistic picture of internal development. Successes were often exaggerated and failures concealed or explained away. News, reports and commentaries from western media could easily be received on the radio and TV and were listened to by many people but were unreliable or untruthful about the GDR.

In the Federal Republic news coverage was obviously part of the psychological warfare proclaimed in 1958 by the minister of defence, Franz Josef Strauss. In the circles in which I moved reports on the GDR from this quarter were not as a rule taken seriously, since they gave a strongly distorted view of life in our country. Frequently lies were published. On 27th August 1958, for example, the important newspaper

Die Welt brought a report on a high-level secret conference in East Berlin on the "increasing flight of scientists" from the GDR to the West. The story had been invented from A to Z: there was no such conference.

On 16th September 1967 the *Frankfurter Allgemeine Zeitung* stated: "It is a fact that the zone taken over (by the Soviet Union – the ed.) in Summer 1945 is one of the least changed areas of Europe." Absurd as this statement was, it shows how far this influential newspaper was prepared to go in its malevolence.

Beyond the Federal Republic the GDR was usually ignored in the media, except for its successes in sports and for the Wall. When I visited England to work in the British Library in 1969 I found that only left-wingers who took a special interest in the GDR knew anything going beyond these two subjects. The deputy headmaster of my old school asked me quite seriously: "What would happen in your street if a coloured man bought a house there?"

He was astonished when I told him that nobody would object, but that it was rarely possible to buy a house. An important source of information for some people was obviously the novel *The Spy Who Came In From The Cold* by John le Carré, published a few years before.

At the same time the foreign policy of the GDR presented us with no problems; it was, as we saw international affairs, just as it should be. There could be no doubt that it contributed, as far as the GDR was able, to international peace and to aid for liberation movements outside Europe. The latter subject interested me more and more in the 1960s and perhaps as a result I tended to pay less attention to internal problems.

As I already mentioned, the closing of the border with West Berlin made life more difficult for Erika and me. With two small children to look after she could not travel to Berlin daily, and in Kleinmachnow there was no work for academics. As a lecturer I earned enough to cover our modest needs and therefore she attached herself to the Institute for East European history of our university and, from home, wrote a doctoral thesis on a notable Soviet historian, going to Berlin once or twice a month to take part in seminars and keep up contacts. But she was socially almost completely isolated in Kleinmachnow, since her sisters and many people she knew had left the settlement. During term I usually had to spend four or five hours daily travelling to Berlin and back on five, sometimes six days every week, leaving home at 7 a.m. or earlier and not returning before 7 p.m. and often later. It was only nine years later, in 1970, that we finally succeeded in getting a flat in Berlin.

To put an end to a situation that handicapped both of us severely and harmed our family life, I had at last to stifle all qualms and take recourse as a last resort to a step I disliked intensely: I asked a former student of mine who had become one of the three deputy secretaries of the university party committee for help. He simply rang up the university administration and shortly after we were offered the choice of two sizeable flats in Berlin. The official who made the offer had for years rejected all applications I had sent him. His turnabout was obviously due to the heightened authority of the party apparatus whose members were now able to give orders or "recommendations" in most spheres of life. They were usually obeyed. Often their interference was justified and sometimes it prevented serious harm. But what troubled me in this case was that it amounted to obtaining a weighty advantage (so weighty that it amounted to a privilege) through the party.

At the department of history I continued my lectures, other teaching and research seemingly with success, and was appointed professor in 1964. But much of the teaching here gradually lost its attraction, because a type of student very different from those I had been used to working with came into the foreground. The students we had in the 1950s studied history and, additionally, languages and philosophy. Most of the students who came to us from the early 1960s onwards studied two disciplines of equal weighting as well as pedagogics.

The change began with a measure we could only applaud. An entirely new educational system had been built up, which was radically different from the system Germany had known before 1945. It was unitary and knew no class distinctions, drawing basic ideas from the German socialist school reformers of the Weimar Republic. The children of generals and secretaries of state sat side by side in class with the children of unskilled labourers. Corporal punishment was strictly prohibited; teachers who resorted to it had to expect disciplinary proceedings. All schools were co-educational. Not only were there concerted efforts to raise the level of village schools to the standard expected in towns, but the elementary school system as a whole had by 1960 reached an obviously higher standard than that of the elementary school I had attended in a middle class district of Berlin in 1927-31. An important new feature was the division into two stages: the lower stage comprised the first four classes, the higher stage the second four. Teachers were trained either for the lower or the higher stage and never taught in both. In the lower they taught all subjects, in the higher two or at the most three. The only serious weakness of many of the elementary schools in towns was poor discipline, presumably due largely to the inexperience of the teachers, most of whom were young. But apparently weak discipline was also widespread in schools in western Europe at the time.

In 1966 our elder son entered school in Kleinmachnow, his younger brother followed two years later. We were greatly impressed by the way things worked out. The teachers were interested in cooperation with parents and did so whenever possible, and we thus came to know our elder son's class teacher quite well. She was a highly trained and skilful guide for the children entrusted to her and distinctly popular among them. The school turned out to be much better than we had expected.

My acquaintance with our educational system at the university was, alas, not so happy. After extensive discussion on educational matters the *Volkskammer* (the parliament) had passed a bill in late 1959 extending compulsory schooling for all children by two years, i.e. a ninth and a tenth class, and including technical instruction in the curriculum. Pupils who intended (and were considered by their teachers to be good enough) to study at a university or other higher institute of science or engineering were, as before, to transfer to an upper school after completing the eighth class. This ambitious programme, pushed through with unwarranted haste, demanded the training of tens of thousands of additional teachers. Until then teachers for elementary schools had been trained exclusively at colleges subordinate to the Ministry of Education, but these colleges were unable to cope with the numbers now needed. Therefore the universities, for whom the State Secretariat for Higher Education was responsible, were called on to train students in large numbers who were intended to teach in the middle level i.e. from the fifth to the tenth class of the new elementary schools.

At the department of history we were therefore confronted in 1960, as has already been mentioned, with many new students who were dividing their time between history, a subject with an equal weighting, and pedagogics. The number of students without pedagogics, the type we had been used to, was reduced. Among the first of this new generation of student teachers, many were keen on teaching history and I was able to recruit a group of them to work on the history of German colonies. This they did with great zeal, and I regretted having to let them go, with laudatory comment on their diplomas. It was the only time that I succeeded in gathering such a group of students teachers; the later students of this category were less motivated for the teaching profession and often had little interest in history. Consequently many were inattentive in lectures.

The staff of our department at first took this to be a passing state of affairs. When it persisted we talked about it with professors of the pedagogics department, most of whom were former headmasters, who tended to ward off critical remarks about students for whom they were administratively responsible. We also sent complaints to the State Secretariat and the Ministry of Education. The representatives of the former understood our dissatisfaction but declared that the ministry was the appropriate authority, the latter never replied to anything we sent. Relations between the two government departments were extremely bad and it was known that their heads hardly communicated with each other.

Soon the reasons for the intolerable situation became evident. Many of these students had not wanted to become teachers at all, but had been rejected for other courses and had then applied with the intention of taking up some other, quite different, work after completing their studies. Others had applied to be trained as teachers of music, sports or fine arts, only to be told that they would be accepted only on condition that they studied history as a second subject. Thus a new type of history student had been created: the *Muß-Historiker* (compulsory historian). The absolutely idiotic combination of history with the subjects mentioned had been invented by the Ministry of Education.

Not only were we confronted with students not interested in history, but these students were in music, fine arts and sports subject to a strict regime of daily exercises as well as lectures and seminars, and therefore had in any case little time for history. Such a regime of daily chores was unknown in our department, where we rejected any "school type" of instruction. We tried to ease the situation by adapting to some extent to the needs of the student teachers. Lectures and seminars for them were held separately from those for other students, seminars reduced to repetition of what had been said in the main lectures, and less difficult questions set in examinations.

However, some professors and lecturers ignored the lower standards and depleted thirst for knowledge of most of their students and then complained about poor attendance and lack of discipline. When, as part of preparations for a joint committee meeting with the department of pedagogics, I went to a lecture given by a colleague and took a seat right at the back of the hall, I found that two groups of students played cards until the lecture ended. Twice I had to throw students out of my own lectures because they kept talking.

During the 1960s my discontent with this state of affairs rose from year to year, all the more so because most of my colleagues, finding their complaints disregarded, became resigned to it, with the result that university professors were engaged in teaching which could have been done just as well, if not better, by young assistants. I had to give up encouraging students into research: the only ones I could now direct to archival sources were my two assistants and some extra-mural MA and PhD candidates. The basic principle of our university, "the unity of reaching and research", had been virtually annulled. At the same time more administrative work was put on my shoulders, much of which consisted of designing programmes for future activities of the faculty of philosophy, to which we all belonged. My drafts turned out to be a waste of time, since the faculty – a huge and absolutely ungovernable body – was abolished a few years after. Had there not been an atmosphere of lively scholarly exchange and debate among staff members, under the guidance of people I liked and respected, my membership of the department would have been ended sooner than it did.

Historians and Historical Science.
The most eminent historians of our university at this time, after the distressing death of Alfred Meusel in 1960, were the following:
Eduard Winter, director of the Institute of Soviet and East European history, was a man of imposing appearance and great personal authority. Born in Bohemia in 1896, the son of an officer of the Austro-Hungarian army, this Catholic theologian and church historian had taught for many years at the theological faculty of the German university in Prague. In 1940 he had given up his holy orders and left this faculty to become professor of the history of ideas at the same university and in 1947 he had accepted the offer of a chair of East European history at the university in Halle in the Soviet Zone of Germany. He had been president at this university from 1948 to 1951, before coming to Berlin as the successor of the renowned Otto Hoetzsch. At our university in the 1950s and 1960s he succeeded in rearing an entire generation of younger historians who were to dominate his field in the GDR. His monthly seminars for doctoral candidates, which I attended whenever I could for the sheer pleasure of watching his inimitable style of dealing with his pupils, were by far the best at the department since Meusel had left. His numerous publications on East European and church history brought him an international reputation.
An exceptional personality of a different kind who gained international standing only in her last years was Elisabeth Welskopf-Henrich.

The daughter of a lawyer, she was born in Munich in 1901 and had studied ancient history, philosophy and economy at Berlin University. Before and during the Second World War she had worked as a statistician, and in the war years joined a communist resistance group, one of whose members she had hidden for a long time at great risk to her life. Appointed lecturer in ancient history at our university in 1952 and professor in 1960, she gained an international reputation as the author of works on leisure in ancient Greece and the history of the Greek polis. She was little known to our students: ancient history was given little room in the curriculum for student teachers and among the others there were only few who took much interest in it. After her official retirement in 1962 she continued her work as a matter of course, as Winter had done. No successor was appointed. When I told the then head of the department, Streisand, that it was a disgrace for a university to whose fame such classical scholars as Theodor Mommsen and Ulrich von Wilamowitz-Moellendorf had contributed to have no professor of ancient history, he could only agree, but did nothing about it, as far as I know. The chair for primeval history (the term "pre-history" was rightly rejected) was, on the other hand, continually held by first-rate internationally recognized experts.

Elisabeth Welskopf-Henrich was a small, inconspicuous, cheerful person, always prepared to listen to a good joke, and at the same time a very hard worker. For several years we belonged to the same party group and became quite good friends who sometimes pursued this or that practical aim in the university together. Her deep understanding of Marxist theory made her an opponent of dogmatic approaches and in discussions in 1966 on the newly published official *History of the German Labour Movement* she warned against regarding it as free from mistakes. She was not only a brilliant scholar but also a successful writer, having published about a dozen novels. At least two of these quickly became best-sellers: *Jan und Jutta*, based on her experiences in the anti-Nazi resistance, and *Die Söhne der großen Bärin*, which dealt with the struggle of North American Prairie Indians against the advancing whites in the second half of the nineteenth century. On journeys to Canada and the United States she came to know the Dakota in their present-day reservations, made friends with the leaders of the Native American movement and supported it with further books. Her novels were written, she told me during one of my visits to her home in Berlin-Treptow, in the evenings: she used to go to bed about 10 p.m. and then wrote for two or three hours before going to sleep.

Joachim Streisand, born in Berlin in 1920 as son of a Jewish bookseller with social-democratic affiliations who was a man of learning in his own right (a type of bookseller once common in Germany but now unfortunately extict), had, though officially classified as "half-Jew", been able to study philosophy, history and other subjects at the universities of Rostock and Berlin up till 1942. He was then expelled from the latter and forced to work in war industries. Imprisoned in a camp for "half-breeds", he escaped to Berlin and hid there until the war ended. As a teacher of history and sociology in evening courses for adults in West Berlin he joined the SED in 1948 and was promptly dismissed. Recommended by Alfred Meusel for a stipend, he joined the small but select group of Meusel's pupils at our university, among whom he soon became conspicuous as the most brilliant. In 1951 he began lecturing on German history in the nineteenth century and in the following years, till his appointment as professor and head of the Institute of German History in 1963, mastered many important tasks: deputy head of the department for the period 1848-95 in the Museum for German History, co-editor of our monthly historical journal, author of the first Marxist outline of German history 1789-1815 and a number of pioneering studies on leading German scholars of the nineteenth century, re-organisation of the Academy of Sciences etc. Streisand was a historian with unusually wide interests, especially for literature and the theatre, a stimulating teacher and a very capable organiser. His contacts with students in the 1960s suffered somewhat, it seemed to me, not only from the circumstances described above but also from the multitude of activities he took upon himself. As a party member he invariably toed the line, obviously regarding himself as being more or less "under orders".

In the 1960s historical research and publication advanced considerably. Some examples for the 20th century: the Institute of History at the Academy of Sciences completed a three-volume history of Germany in the First World War, edited by Fritz Klein. Walter Markov, still in Leipzig, had begun in 1959 to publish numerous studies on African and colonial history, which found a climax in his contribution to the Moscow International Congress of Historians in 1970. Horst Drechsler's basic study of German rule in Namibia was published (later it was translated into English, Russian and Portuguese) as was the also basic study by my friend Friedrich Katz, who was also at our institute, on German policy in Mexico 1870-1920 and Günter Rosenfeld's book on German-Soviet relations 1917-1922. Dietrich Eichholtz and Wolfgang Schumann began with their publications of

In Dakar, December 1967. Front: Irmgard Sellnow. Top, in the middle: Walter Markov

documents on the policy of German banks and trusts before and during the Second World War. At the University of Rostock my friend Johannes Nichtweiss had initiated research on agrarian history in the preceding years. After his untimely death in 1958 I edited his manuscript on foreign (mostly Polish) seasonal workers in East German agriculture 1890-1914 and published it. His pupil Lothar Elsner took up the subject of foreign workers in Germany with further studies.

It would be going too far to deal with all the discussions among the historians of the GDR during these years. Some of the most important ones were about the character of the revolution of 1918-19 in Germany (in the late 1950s, initiated by Albert Schreiner). Was it bourgeois-democratic or socialist? Other dealt with such subjects as: Were the Reformation and the Peasants' War in Germany an "early bourgeois revolution"? Were the relations of production in the pre-colonial states of West and East Africa feudal or were they examples of the Asiatic mode of production Marx had discovered? Was the Asiatic mode of production a "mode" in its own right, to be recognized as equal in status with the mode of slavery? Was Dimitrov's definition of fascism as the openly terrorist dictatorship of the most reactionary, chauvinist and imperialist elements of finance capital really adequate?

The manifold publications were evidence of the lively and productive atmosphere pervading the historical institutes of the GDR. But there were weaknesses, some avoidable, some inevitable. Since many of the younger historians (and the editors in publishing houses) were products of the cultural revolution, many publications could not claim literary quality. All too few biographies were written before 1970. The only ones worth mentioning dealt with Luther, Engels, Bebel and Mehring. This was obviously partly due to the revulsion against the worship of heroes and leaders characteristic of the Nazi regime and nationalistic historiography before it, but also to a certain helplessness regarding the psychology of people who lived in other periods than our own. But it seemed to me that the most serious weaknesses could well have been avoided. With the introduction of standardised study programmes in 1951-2 the division of modern history into three parts had been introduced, copying the example of Soviet universities, which in practice meant that German history was taught not as part of European or world history but isolated from them. Students were therefore often unable to recognize the import or significance of developments in Germany for other peoples or humanity as a whole or, conversely, the influence of world history on historical events and processes in Germany.

A further weakness to be found occasionally was a tendency on the part of some historians to impose Marxist theoretical concepts on living history in a mechanical fashion, thereby violating not only historical reality but also the views of the inventors of those concepts.

Achievements and contradictions.

During our disputes, doubts, worries, and fits of resignation we never lost sight of the historical achievements which the GDR could be justly proud of. When I complained to my mother about the sometimes unbelievable stupidity and blindness of the higher ranks of our leadership and the subaltern, narrow spirit of subordination widespread in the lower ranks, she would reply: "You must keep in mind, my boy, that these are *our* people, and that our state is very young. For how many generations have the *Junker* (big landowners) and the bourgeoisie ruled in Germany?" She died in 1966, nearly 70 years old. I did not forget her admonitions.

Despite of the critical situations that arose from time to time – the plans for 1969 and 1970, for example, were not fulfilled – the economy had made impressive advances and the standard of living had risen. Considerable investments had been made to increase the numbers of

74

highly trained technical and scientific personnel in industry and to introduce the most modern equipment. The quality of industrial products had improved and exports were rising. But industry remained largely dependent on raw materials imported from abroad.

There was a fairly well functioning network of cooperatively owned, state and private shops for all types of consumer goods. But the standard of salesmanship was and, alas, remained low; no trader needed to worry that he would be unable to sell his stocks, and saleswomen were badly trained and poorly paid. Nowhere was the customer treated like a king. The prices for food and other cheaper wares for daily consumption were extremely cheap, being heavily subsidised, while more expensive goods (high quality clothes, cars, television sets etc.) were very expensive. These more expensive goods were often scarce or lacking, with the result that people travelled around to find them. When they were delivered to a shop, queues would often spring up quickly.

Since 1960 virtually all farmers, small, medium, and wealthy, belonged to agricultural production cooperatives. These cooperatives and the state farms were, not without success, encouraged to operate jointly wherever this would bring better results. The consequences were salutary: by 1967 all eggs and milk and nearly all meat and butter needed were produced by our own farms.

An obviously serious handicap was the relatively (in comparison with the Federal Republic) low productivity of labour in important branches of industry and other fields of employment, where strict control was difficult or impossible, or the type of work did not require constant exertion, or attention. This was particularly evident in the building trade, notorious for wasting materials and not fulfilling plan targets. Pedestrians passing building sites were almost certain to notice workers waiting for instructions, or killing time because the material they needed had not arrived. In the 1960s office staff in many had places become accustomed to not working hard since no one forced them to. Although there were constant attempts to change this state of affairs in industry, there was not much improvement, as far as I could see. It was rarely dealt with in the media.

There were several reasons for the relatively low productivity of labour. An important one was that the demand for labour was higher than the supply. There was no unemployment. A worker who disliked the job he had and left it could easily find another. A further reason was that the labour legislation made it very difficult to dismiss an employee. The trade union organisation at the place of work had to consent to every dismissal in its sphere. If it consented, the person dismissed could begin proceedings at a court of law. Unless the employer proved that there were really serious grounds for the dismissal, such as constant absence from work or theft of socialist property, the court would usually decide in favour of the plaintiff. One of the directors of the university administration once told me that among the 8,000 university employees there were about 30 who should for various reasons have been discharged. The university was keeping them, however, because the amount of red tape and court proceedings involved in getting rid of them would mean far too great expense.

The introduction of the five day working week in 1967 did not, it seemed, affect economic development much. (At our university it only benefited secretaries and other employees; there had been no teaching on Saturdays for years.) At the same time the minimum monthly wage was increased to 300 Marks and the minimum annual holiday to 15 days. Families with many children received a substantial monthly state bonus.

Really impressive was the system of social security; there were no beggars or homeless people, and the department for social matters in every district saw to it that no one starved or froze. Rents for flats and houses were extremely cheap; they often amounted to less than one tenth of a family's income. Since these low maximum rents were fixed by law (according to the size and quality of the accommodation rented) and the owner had to pay maintenance and repair costs, the private ownership of houses brought virtually no profits and privately owned houses – of which there were many – were not often sold. (The official attitude to people who did not pay their rent was unbelievably lax. In many cities it was possible not to pay for years without being evicted.) But accommodation was in short supply and could only be obtained through the local authority, which had to decide who could move into vacant flats or houses. There were long lists of applicants, and the danger of bribery of officials and preferred treatment of friends and relations was met by strict control of all decisions through local committees consisting of non-official persons.

A serious weakness were the very small monthly pensions – pittances would be the fitting expression – received by the majority of old people. Even if the "second invisible income" every citizen benefited from is taken into account, these sums could stand no comparison with the pensions paid in the Federal Republic. It was virtually impossible to subsist on them without assistance from relations or others. For members of professions with a higher income, especially academics, higher pensions were gradually introduced since the early 1950s.

On the other hand the comprehensive system of social insurance provided nearly everyone with medical treatment by practitioners, in clinics and in hospitals without payment. Medicine prescribed by a doctor was also "free", as were spectacles, unless a superior type of frame was ordered, and medical aids of all kinds, including false teeth. Everyone in employment received 90 per cent of his wages for up six weeks annually in case of illness with a doctor's certificate. If the illness lasted longer 70 per cent was paid. There were only very few doctors with a private practice; practitioners were nearly all employed in clinics, hospitals, or state practices. I cannot remember ever paying a single Pfennig for medical purposes for my family or myself during the forty years the GDR existed, with one exception. When my wife incurred a serious skin ailment and several doctors had not been able to help, I sent her to the best specialist available, the director of the dermatological clinic of the Charité, our university's huge medical centre, who accepted her as a private patient for a fee of 100 Marks.

But neither old age pensions nor medical treatment were "free of charge". Up to a monthly wage or salary of 600 Marks 10 per cent was deducted for insurance; earnings above this sum were disregarded for this calculation. For the self-employed, such as private shopkeepers (of whom there were many), insurance was voluntary. One could also insure one's property or life, if one wished.

Medical services and old age pensions could not be financed from insurance payments alone and were heavily subsidised from the state budget.

All stages of education were free of charge, from admission to the crèche and the kindergarten to university finals, as well as vocational training. Exceptions were private lessons in, say, music, or for children who had not attended school because of illness, or were weak in this or that subject. But these lessons were usually given by teachers or parents of other children without charge. Education at schools maintained by the churches was also not free, but such schools were few and far between. Fees paid for private instruction were a purely private matter, as we found when we sent our elder son to a harpist for lessons. In the 1950s the universities demanded fees from students whose parents had an exceptionally high income, but this practice was discontinued in the 1960s. After that all students (except for a few foreigners) were paid a monthly stipend sufficient to cover basic expenses. Some but not many earned additional money by working during evenings or their holidays, a practice teaching staff would discourage because study results could easily suffer as a result. A PhD degree would also cost the candidate nothing, unless he entered for it privately, without connection with the university concerned.

The legal system had not only been thoroughly reformed and brought into accord with socialist principles but also much simplified in order to make it understandable for everyone. Petty offences and small conflicts were not dealt with by courts of justice but by the conflict commissions in larger places of employment and commissions of arbitration in city districts, both voluntary bodies consisting of people delegated by the trade unions, the women's league and other organisations. Conflict commissions usually dealt with small offences, complaints and clashes at places of work, the arbitration commissions with conflicts in residential areas and dwelling-houses. Some petty offences did not even get that far. One day a police sergeant turned up at our sub-department and informed us that the librarian who worked for us, an elderly lady without much training, had been caught shoplifting in a supermarket. The sergeant asked us to speak seriously with her and return to the police a form he gave us, on which we were to confirm that we had done so. We fulfilled his request.

The principle underlying the whole system was the education of offenders, not their punishment. Criminal offences had to be really serious for the accused, if found guilty, to be sent to prison. Had they served their term (which was usually reduced if the danger of new offences was considered small) they were, on release, looked after by local authorities. These saw to it that they found work and accommodation, a task which was often a source of conflict, since usually neither firms nor workers wanted to have them. Sometimes the employment of released ex-prisoners had to be enforced by administrative order. And when they were given newly built flats there were understandable protests from people who had been waiting for a flat for months or years. On the whole there was much less litigation than is customary in western countries, and correspondingly the number of lawyers in private practice was small. Most people who had studied law worked for the state administration or for socialist enterprises as advisers. It was, of course, quite impossible for a lawyer to become rich by defending wealthy people accused in court.

One feature of the legal system was undemocratic. No citizen could take legal action against a state agency; what he could do was to send an *Eingabe* (something between a complaint and a petition) to the superior of the person or organ his complaint was about, or to the complaints commission of the district or the regional representative body, or to authorities above them right up to the chairman of the state council. Such *Eingaben* had by law to be replied to and if possible dealt with within four weeks. Usually, but not always, this law was complied with, naturally not always to the satisfaction of the petitioner.

The constitution adopted in 1968 stated in Article 20 (2): "Men and women have equal rights and have the same legal status in all spheres of social, state and personal life. The promotion of women, particularly with regard to vocational qualifications, is a task of society and the state." Since the early 1960s the advancement of the female sex had been put on the agenda by the leaders of the SED, and in 1965 a whole set of laws on the family had been adopted for this purpose. Equal pay for equal work was a basic principle: no woman could be paid less than a man for the job she was doing. At this time about 75 per cent of all women were employed, full or part time, and the percentage was to rise still further. There were very extensive efforts to train women for more qualified work in industry, since the percentage continued to be low in positions which required some training.

But progress was not rapid, mainly, I suppose, because in Germany looking after the household and after children was traditionally, more than in Britain or the United States, the women's lot. To alleviate it and to enable more women to take up a job, the number of kindergartens and créches was continually being increased.

At the university the percentage of female students was high in the 1960s and they were not at all different from the male of their species, with one exception: the proportion of drop-outs was higher. Women were numerous among assistants, but their number was much smaller among lecturers and very small among professors. Persistent efforts by the Ministry of Higher Education to raise the percentage of female scholars only resulted very gradually in changes. When promotions were being considered membership of the female sex was always an advantage. On one occasion in the late 1960s ten women lecturers at Leipzig university were appointed extraordinary professors by the ministry at one go. Perhaps there were similar steps at other universities, but this was the only one I ever heard about. All universities and other bodies employing large numbers of women had *Frauen-förderungskommissionen* (Commissions for the advancement of women), which looked after female interests in close contact with the trade union committees. They often dealt with complaints by women who thought that they had been discriminated against or not properly treated. But most of all they engaged in putting pressure on department heads or directors to delegate more women to vocational training courses.

A branch of the economy everyone depended on were the craftsmen and repair services. In our experience in Kleinmachnow and later in Berlin bakers, butchers, hairdressers and shoemakers were always to hand, but it was often difficult to find people willing and able to carry out repairs on housing or on cars. Generally it was best to engage someone who did the job "unofficially" in his spare time or a pensioner, without receipts for the fees paid.

The traditional status of craftsmen with businesses of their own, who had for centuries played an essential part in economy in general and town life in particular (hairdressers, shoemakers, bakers, butchers, plumbers, tailors, watchmakers etc.), was fully maintained. To establish a business they needed, like before 1945, a licence from the local authority which was only granted if they had a master's certificate, if the local chamber of trade consented and their police record was clean. In the 1950s they were gradually placed under the strict controls of the planned economy, which meant that they were allotted the materials and the apprentices they needed by their local economic administration. If the materials they received "legally" did not suffice, they would usually resort to buying from illicit sources. Those I came to know often complained of insufficient or poor supplies or tools, or of taxes being too high, but it was suspected that many resorted to double bookkeeping. I never heard of one giving up because of taxation.

After 1960-1 there was a concerted effort to combine these various craftsmen in cooperatives, which in most trades won a leading position in their locality, since the authorities favoured them. Their members received a basic fixed wage and in addition a share in the cooperative's earnings determined by their hours of work or the number of customers they had served. Sometimes craftsmen were put under pressure to join the cooperative of their trade by the local authority, who usually tended to regard independent craftsmen as relics of capitalism. If, say, a shoemaker with a shop of his own was found to have made false income returns in order to pay less taxes the department of trade would let him know that he would not be prosecuted if he joined. And the cooperative won a new member. But many of these people preferred to stay independent, although they had no chance of rising to be small capitalist entrepreneurs. Most of them had a standard of life considerably higher than the average citizen, and they remained a specific social group which tended to be politically passive.

Political differences.

A few months after the 6th Congress of the SED (1963), in which Khrushchev took part, the government proclaimed a "New Economic System of Planning and Management", which devolved more responsibility and independence to the 82 Associations of People's Own Enterprises and their workers. The latter were to participate directly in economic successes. These and other economic reforms soon proved their worth: in the following year the productivity of labour rose by 7 per cent and the national income by 5 per cent. The average living standard rose perceptibly, without reaching that of the Federal Republic. (Our own standard rose even more, but mainly for another reason. I had never cared much about the level of my salary, since we managed to get along modestly, but its rise with my promotion to Professor without a Chair in 1964 did make quite a difference. We were now able to buy a TV set and then a good car of the Soviet "Moskvitch" type.)

But since the dismissal of Khrushchev in Moscow in October 1964 the upward trend of the economy, coupled with more democracy in the factories and workshops, was not accompanied by more real democracy in everyday politics. Bureaucracy gained more power in public life and in the SED. The decisive position of the SED, and its mutation to a party with ever increasing centralism in decision-making and gradually dwindling self-determination of the membership became more marked. This was shown, *inter alia*, by the expansion of the body of full-time party officials: the "party worker", in the 1950s often a member of another profession or trade and engaged only temporarily, was now in many cases recruited when still young, trained for long-time activity in this field and permanently employed.

It was in these years that I first heard the ugly word *apparatchik*. It is, at any rate for the GDR, inappropriate, since these men and women were not simply cogs in a machine, although they developed in that direction later. Usually of working class origin and often coming from families connected with the labour movement for generations, they were not, as a rule, bureaucrats or administrators. They were political guides, advisers, and controllers. The discipline demanded of them was stricter than for ordinary party members but not as strict as that of the corps of professional revolutionaries at the head of the German Communist Party in the Weimar Republic, which had been almost military, and not to be compared with that enforced on Roman Catholic clerics. Their salaries were not high, certainly not higher than the salaries they could have earned in other professions. As for the privileges they were often accused in Western countries of enjoying, in the 1960s they were, with few exceptions, hardly substantial.

Like all bodies of professional people with a higher training the SED had holiday homes reserved for its employees, at which they could spend their annual leave. The canteens to be found in party institutions offered more goods in short supply than the canteens in other places – the staff canteen of the Institute of Marxism-Leninism of the Central Committee, whose excellent library contained books not to be found elsewhere in the GDR, was better than that at Humboldt University as I found when occasionally lunching there. This practice had been inherited from the Soviet administration, which had after the war insisted on supplementing the rations for certain categories of people. Here, as in other spheres, the truth of Max Weber's dictum on "the power of established habit to serve as norm" was confirmed. In the press this subject remained taboo. There were local variations as to holiday homes, canteens and other smaller privileges, which were sometimes changed or abolished by the locally responsible party chief.

A really important advantage "party workers" shared with other groups closely tied to the socialist regime, and with people treated more preferentially than anyone else, such as prominent scientists, artists, writers etc., was that their children could often gain admission to university more easily than the normal run of applicants. This practice was not covered by any law or ordinance, but, like other practices that basically did not conform to socialism, simply crept in. It was much disliked at our university, where the staff members dealing with applications for admission from such young people at the various departments often rejected them. The fathers concerned usually protested to the Ministry of Higher Education which, if the applicant's school leaving certificate showed that he or she fulfilled the requirements demanded for the branch of studies wished for, might recommend that the applicant be accepted. (It had no power to order, but a recommendation from this quarter came near to an instruction.) During the three years in which I had to interview applicants for non-pedagogical studies at the department of history, there was, luckily, no such case, but my successor in this task once complained bitterly to me about the trouble she was having with the daughter of an area party secretary.

The development of the university party committee between the late 1950s and the late 1970s reflected, to some degree, changes that took place in the SED. As First Secretary Hans Singer had been much liked and respected; it was known that he got on well with the *Rektoren* (Vice

Chancellors), all non-party men, at the head of the university during his time in office. A chemist by profession, he returned to chemistry on giving up his party position. His successor Werner Tzschoppe had studied philosophy and returned to the job after completing a two-year course in Marxism-Leninism for advanced students in Moscow at the time Khrushchev was at the head of the Soviet Union. When Robert Havemann put forward his ideas at the university in 1963-4 Tzschoppe supported him and was therefore dismissed from his party position, forbidden to enter university buildings and given work as a translator at the Academy of Sciences. I had not much liked what I saw of and heard about him personally, but he had quite a following at the university.

In 1964 the university party committee was given the status of a *Kreisleitung* (district leadership) directly subordinate to the Berlin district leadership of the SED. As before, it had a First Secretary and three other full-time Secretaries (for organisation, science policy, and propaganda), but its office staff and the number of full-time political employees and assistants increased considerably in the following years.

The man who replaced Tzschoppe, Herbert Eissrig, had been trained as an engineer. He never attempted, as far as I know, to take part in theoretical or political discussions within the party. In appearance and manners he might have been a sailor from the merchant navy, but he had been a government official. Unassuming and kindly by nature, he was, as I was told by people who knew him well, quite aware that he was not qualified for his position which he had been persuaded by higher party officials, perhaps with some moral pressure, to accept. He was lucky in having two excellent *Rektoren* as partners: the professor for American literature Karlheinz Wirzberger (the most popular head the university had in my time) and the noted socialist educationalist Helmut Klein. When, after quite a long time, he gave up his position as First Secretary, he was given a leading position in the administration of the university.

His successor, who did not serve for long, had been First Secretary of the Free German Youth at the university. He, too, was not a scholar and took on the position of Head of Cultural Affairs in the city council of East Berlin when he left. The last First Secretary at the university Harry Smettan also lacked an academic background. But unlike Herbert Eissrig he evidently regarded this as an advantage for a "party worker" dealing with academic party members, whom he habitually addressed in a very loud voice. On the few occasions on which I heard him speak my impression was that he had no ideas of his own whatsoever, was endowed with great self-assurance, and was basically anti-intellectual. The great increase in the number of full-time "party workers" – not only at our university – was due to some extent to the steady rise in the number of members. The decisive reason, however, was the decision of the 6th Party Congress in 1963 to give the party "apparatus" control and supervision of the state and economic administration not simply in general but also in detail. From now on no town mayor or director of any enterprise could ignore instructions from his district or area party head committee, whether he belonged to the party or not, if he wished to keep his job. The result, as far as I could see, was on the one hand, greater efficiency and uniformity, but on the other less initiative and personal authority on the part of local state officials and of managers. Some later said of the heads of area and district administrations that they had "lost their faces" and that the man who counted was the First Secretary; others told me that the mayor remained *the* man in town whom the inhabitants looked to to settle their complaints while the first secretary was known only to party members. Evidently there were regional differences; changes here, as in other spheres, were gradual.

About this time discipline for party members became more rigorous. Attendance at the monthly meetings held by each local organisation was now a duty not to be ignored light-heartedly. At the beginning of each meeting the chairman would state who was excused or had to leave before the end for legitimate reasons. If the reason given by the member for leaving seemed insufficient permission to do so was refused by the presiding board; if the matter was doubtful it was put to the vote. The member in question – usually a young woman with children to look after – had to accept the result. Members also had to participate in the huge public demonstrations held every year on May 1st (International Labour Day) and October 7th (anniversary of the foundation of the GDR), both public holidays. These two demonstrations became almost compulsory for everyone working or studying, with the result that they largely lost their character as inspiring and mobilising events. Masses of people turned up at these demonstrations and walked along passively without showing a trace of sentiment. Others turned up so that their attendance could be taken note of and then returned home as soon as they could, long before the demonstration was over. This lack of keenness or even willingness to demonstrate on these occasion was by no means true of all taking part – I remember many of these demonstrations at which the university people and many, many others were in the best of spirits, especially if the weather was good. But it was evident enough to deeply disappoint a group of Austrian Young Communists, whose acquaintance I made one May 1st in the late 1960s.

A similar decline of a ritual observed listlessly by many of those taking part had begun (if my memory does not err) even earlier with regard to the general elections which took place every two years, alternately to the central parliament (*Volkskammer*) and the area and district councils. Since there were no candidates contending with each other, or disputed issues, it was really a vote for or against the "National Front" in which all five parties, the trade unions, the Free German Youth and other smaller organisations were united. The "National Front" always called on voters to cast their vote openly by throwing the list of candidates they had been given on entering the polling stations into the ballot-box in full view of the polling board. Therefore only a small minority retired behind a curtain to mark their paper by crossing out some or all candidates. A larger minority simply stayed away.

Since the party leaders laid great stress on results of 97 or 98 per cent in favour of the "National Front", the local party organisations were in charge of calling on those who had not voted by about lunch time and persuading them to do so. Often with success. My colleagues and I thought that this whole business, which in the course of the years degenerated into an empty formality, was quite stupid, but could not say so publicly. Among students the elections were sarcastically called "a population census". We asked ourselves and each other what sense there was in the unbelievably high rate of votes for the policies of the SED, in many places obtained by the application of mild and polite (moral) pressure. They could either show that 98 per cent of our population supported the policies of the SED, which was obviously not the case (c. 70 per cent would have been closer to reality), or that the grip of our party and state on its citizens had assumed Orwellian totality, which was also far from the truth. In party and trade union meetings the matter was brought forward from this or that angle again and again since the 1960s, but to no avail.

In 1963 a notable physicist, Robert Havemann, began putting forward his ideas on socialism and GDR politics in his university institute, which soon brought him into conflict with the party leadership. He was a highly respected figure, having taken part in the resistance to Nazism and been sentenced to death during the war, joining the Communist Party in 1945 and then playing a prominent part in the peace movement. At the university, discussion of his lectures did not, as far as I remember, go at first far beyond a circle of followers who assembled around him. This was evidently because he was a poor debater and somewhat helpless when confronted with the task of orally defending his opinions. In philosophy he engaged in sharp attacks on the dogmatic interpretations of Marx, Engels and Lenin then still much in vogue; in politics he demanded far more democracy for all GDR citizens. Gradually the number of students attending his lectures grew and, since he stuck firmly to his opinions, the SED leaders had him expelled from the party and dismissed from his chair by the Minister of Higher Education early in 1964.

At our department he was regarded as a meritorious natural scientist and fighter against Nazism, but, like other natural scientists who had come forward with ideas of their own, weak in Marxist theory and unrealistic in politics. Discussion of Havemann's ideas remained limited in scope in the GDR because they were not published, neither in the party press nor anywhere else in the republic. Some years after he had been expelled he retired to a village near Berlin and until his death in 1982 wrote books and articles which were published in the Federal Republic. By not emigrating there – which he undoubtedly could have done – he demonstrated that he still regarded the GDR as the better of the two German states.

The historians of the GDR took very little notice of him and I do not think any of our students went to his lectures. Since the party leaders had described him as a revisionist he was regarded as an outcast. Had not Bernstein also described socialism as a road and not as the first stage of communism? And had not the revisionists, in our opinion, led the German socialist movement into its worst defeats? The social democrat leaders imbued with revisionist ideas had been guilty of the betrayal of 1914, when instead of opposing the war they had supported the imperial government. They had in 1918-9 prevented government by the workers' and soldiers' councils and seen to it that capitalism was not overthrown and they had in 1932-3 refused to cooperate with the communists against the Nazis and thus made Hitler's accession to power possible.

In 1963 I was concentrating my energies on the higher degree (*Habilitation*) which was demanded for promotion to the rank of professor and cannot remember paying any attention to Havemann, whom I had never seen. On reading some of his articles recently I felt deep regret at not having examined his ideas earlier. Some of his propositions could obviously not be supported, but the direction of his strivings was such that they could well have served as starting point for a constructive discussion of socialism and democracy in the GDR.

That there was no such discussion may well be regarded as the first great sin of omission of the intellectuals of our republic. It might – who knows – even have impelled the nimble Ulbricht not to fall in line with Brezhnev's fatal policies so unreservedly.

Unlike the dispute with Havemann the events in Czechoslovakia in 1968 gave rise to sharp controversy in our department. Developments in Prague, which were discussed in the party press and at several meetings of our party organisation, had drawn much attention to that country in the spring of that year. The party leaders were obviously afraid that the "Prague reformers", who had won a majority in their central committee in April, were leading their country into a repetition of developments in Hungary in 1956, and described them as "right wing revisionists".

In June I was invited by an acquaintance in Kleinmachnow to a private discussion with a radio commentator from Prague, who defended the reformers with the argument that the Czech people would support them. But he was unable to answer to the question what these reforms would mean for the socialist camp as a whole, seeing as the Soviet leaders were trying so hard to convince Dubcek and his associates that they were on the wrong road. Those present agreed with the speaker that changes were needed, since after 1948 Czechoslovakia had copied Soviet policies more closely than the GDR had done and than was good for its economy. But what these changes should be remained unclear. No one expected an intervention by the other powers of the Warsaw Pact.

When the military intervention of the 21st of August took place we were all on holiday. After term had begun, in late September, there was a party meeting at which several party members protested strongly against this step. A professor who had belonged to the Sudeten German minority in Czechoslovakia in his youth and had maintained close ties with that country was especially outraged. A female assistant argued that no socialist country had the right to intervene in such a manner in another, but was opposed by other speakers who stressed that leading Czech communists had been requested the intervention and that the security of the socialist camp must always come first. Unfortunately discussion in the following days and weeks centred on this point, not on what the reforms planned in Prague really meant. My opinion, put forward at the meeting and in the ensuing discussions, was that we could not condemn the political ideas of the Czech reformers without having studied their documents – which were not available to us – thoroughly, but that if, say, six men, were rowing a boat in a race and one of them got up on his feet and started to argue with the others, he had to be pulled down again, if the race were not to be hopelessly lost.

Discussions died down, at least outwardly, after a few weeks. When one of my colleagues at a staff meeting remarked: "We have delivered the counter-revolution in Prague a blow from which we won't recover for a long time", there was an embarrassed silence. Probably the fact that the professor who had protested was, after the university party committee had unsuccessfully tried to make him retract his opinion, struck off the membership list (not expelled) and transferred to a research job at the Academy of Sciences, intimidated the other critics. At no time had there been a serious discussion of the ideas of the Prague reformers; the visits of a number of leading western politicians such as Scheel and Brzezinski to Czechoslovakia to contact politicians and intellectuals sufficed to label the reformers as a danger to socialism.

In the GDR, events in Prague were discussed only among intellectuals; in the factories and among the population in general things had remained quiet. Had our troops been involved in any fighting this might well have been different, but, as transpired later, only a few staff officers actually crossed the border. I was told afterwards that Soviet regiments moving towards Czechoslovakia were cheered by many people in the villages they passed through. Memories of the Czech crisis of 1968 somehow underwent a process of psychological repression. I cannot remember these events even being mentioned subsequently.

The late 1960s at the Humboldt University.

In 1968 my colleagues and I were hard at work applying to our department the third university reform initiated the year before. It brought some notable improvements: the old Philosophical Faculty was dissolved and replaced by a large number of *Sektionen* (departments) with a director with far-reaching powers as head of each. The departments were divided into institutes and sub-departments of varying sizes. New study programmes were introduced and research projects were, if at all possible, to combine several disciplines. The salaries of assistants were increased considerably.

But the preponderance of students for the teaching profession, under the conditions described above, remained. It is difficult to say to what extent this contributed to the deterioration of the general atmosphere at our department which now set in. The main reason may well have been the stultifying effect of the turn in party policy on the social sciences after the intervention in Czechoslovakia, which could be clearly observed in our sub-department of modern history. Another reason was that controls from above became stricter and some of the best scholars left the department. My colleague and good friend Friedrich Katz, an excellent Austrian specialist in Latin American history, returned to his native Vienna after telling me in confidence that he profoundly disagreed with the intervention. Others transferred to the Academy of Sciences.

Although I was appointed to a Professorship with Chair in 1968, shortly after having been made head of the sub-department of modern general history, I became distinctly dissatisfied. In spite of my objections the sub-department was given the official designation "Sub-department for modern general history and history of the socialist and labour movement". This meant that the field I worked on with the help of two assistants, colonial history and history of Africa, was reduced to a sideline. It was a stupid decision, since it was clear that the history of socialism was primarily the domain of the research institutes of the SED, and that these institutes would involve our sub-department in endless discussions and impose their will on it.

I did not comply with the demands of the director, Streisand, that I exercise a constant strict control over all members of my sub-department. Thereby I not only provoked his criticism but drew the wrath of one of the secretaries of the university party committee, Mohrmann, on my head. Some time before I had clearly annoyed the committee by opposing and bringing to naught a resolution against the alleged views of a colleague, the philosopher Wolfgang Heise. The resolution had been submitted to a specially convened meeting of all professors of the Philosophical Faculty who were party members by another of the secretaries, who said that Heise's views were far removed from the current party line and a danger. Heise was absent from Berlin and as first speaker I had simply said that we could not possibly reject his opinions without having heard him. (I have forgotten what they were about.) After this Mohrmann, who had been assigned to see to it that the "party line" was observed in our department organisation, and whom I much disliked because of the hectoring, almost intimidating tone of his speeches at party meetings, treated me with distrust.

In 1969 he and the director began to criticise me because of "negligence" and "liberalism", and in the following year I was dismissed as head of the sub-department. The criticism had been justified inasmuch as I always put teaching and research first and administrative duties second, but it was exaggerated and unduly sharp. I did not regret being rid of a position in which I had lost interest after the profile of the sub-department had been so radically modified. However, the reaction of my colleagues offended and wounded me; with the exception of one of my assistants (the other was in Africa) none of them expressed regret or said anything in my favour. Their passive acceptance and support for decisions made "above" smacked of the old and bad, deeply undemocratic German *Untertanengeist* (spirit of humble submissiveness to authority), which here had undergone an unholy merger with party discipline. My employment as professor was not affected, but I now began to look for another position.

One day the director of the Department of Asian (and African) Studies of our university asked me if I could name an experienced historian who might be willing to teach historical method and colonial history at his department. The professors working there were nearly all philologists, linguists, specialists on Asiatic or African literature or economy and he would need an historian with a broader profile especially to supervise postgraduates preparing dissertations on history. To his surprise I immediately told him: "I'm the man you're looking for", and in 1971, after overcoming some bureaucratic hurdles, joined his department.

The leadership.

In May 1971 Ulbricht resigned as First Secretary. He was nearly 78 years old, and the reason he gave as "old age" may well have been among the true grounds. But there was evidently more to it than that. There were great difficulties in industry and agriculture; the winter of 1969-70 had been exceptionally hard and long and the plan for 1970 had not been fulfilled. In addition, attempts to introduce cybernetics into industrial management had created much confusion. The possibilities inherent in the resources of the republic had been generally over-estimated.

Ulbricht had evidently lost the unreserved support from Moscow he had until then been able to count on. In 1967 he had realised that it would not do to adhere as closely to Soviet ideas and policies as had been done since 1956. He put forward the new theory that socialism was not just a short transitory stage of social development but a socio-economic system in its own right (implying that communism, where everyone's income was to be determined by his or her needs, was still a long way off). This theoretical innovation differed from the official theory advocated by the CPSU; it was evidently intended to bring official theory into accord with obvious reality. It was not accepted in Moscow and may well have contributed to his downfall.

With the election of his successor, Erich Honecker, a turning point in GDR history had been reached, as seems clearer today than it did then. In important respects, at first almost imperceptible, processes of decline set in about this time, and it is difficult not to bring them into some connection with the new First Secretary, who had been youth leader until 1955 and later in the Politburo Secretary for Security.

At the university not much notice was taken of his election. One event left a bad impression. The economic historian Kuczynski published a sickening article on the new first secretary, flattering him in sycophantic terms. He revealed that Honecker had seen to it that he, Kuczynski, was given an institute of economic history of his own at the Academy of Sciences. At our department we were all disgusted. Who the hell was Honecker to interfere in this way in Academy affairs? He could not possibly judge whether Kuczynski should be given a department or an institute to direct.

Gradually it became evident that Honecker was in many respects different from his predecessor. Ulbricht had been a very poor speaker; Honecker was no speaker at all. Whenever he had to make a speech, whether important or not, he pulled out a piece of paper and read whatever was written on it, carefully not deviating from the text. Ulbricht had from time to time visited one of our universities and talked with professors and students on political matters; Honecker during his whole eighteen years as head of the SED never, as far as I remember, did the same. The first chairman of the party, Pieck, never missed the première of a play by Brecht at that poet's theatre; Ulbricht and his wife frequently visited one of the East Berlin theatres; Honecker never, to my knowledge, followed their example. He only liked to attend the official unveiling of major buildings or monuments which had been re-built or newly erected. The only novel he ever publicly praised, as far as I remember, was a somewhat lurid story published in 1976 by a well-known author of espionage and adventure stories, Harry Thürk, based on the career of Solzhenitsyn, who was pictured as an unwitting tool of the CIA. Neither Thürk nor anyone else would have claimed literary merits for the novel, but Honecker declared it to be exemplary.

Ulbricht had on several occasions shown genuine interest in history and in his speeches he sometimes alluded to historical personalities or events. Honecker had no such interests; he was not particularly interested in Marxist theory either and hardly ever alluded to it. After he had been in office for some years most of us had the impression that he was, in reality, more of a figurehead than anything else. Ulbricht always had a touch of the controversial about him; Honecker was simply uninteresting.

At first he seems to have occupied himself with various fields in turn, for theoretically he was responsible for everything. But finding that the problems of GDR economy were beyond his grasp, he delegated them to the leading economist in the Politburo*, Günter Mittag, who in the 1970s and 1980s ruled virtually supreme in this sphere. A clear division of labour developed. Internal policy was dealt with by the head of the government, Willi Stoph, and increasingly by the Minister of State Security, Erich Mielke (member of the Politburo since 1976), party affairs by Horst Dohlus, education by Honecker's wife Margot (not a member of the Politburo), ideology, culture and science by Kurt Hager. For himself Honecker reserved foreign policy, with Hermann Axen as his aide, and the media with Joachim Herrmann (after 1978) as his as-

*The Politburo was, together with the Secretariat of the Central Committee, the highest leading body of the SED. It made all decisions of general significance.

sistant. The latter was a man of mediocre intellect quite incapable of having any ideas of his own.

At our department there was now little genuine respect for the Politburo. We – as almost the entire party membership – imagined that its members worked in daily contact with each other, that they were a genuine socialist team. Only after the collapse of the GDR it became clear that they were nothing of the sort. Mittag, for example, had a personal monopoly of all economic statistics and decided, without consulting his colleagues, which figures were published and which were not.

In spite of its poor leadership, the GDR had important successes in the 1970s. The gradual rise in material living standards continued, even if the increasing pressure to export to non-socialist countries led to noticeable gaps in the supply of goods. One year, for example, it was almost impossible to obtain towels and tablecloths – the entire production was obviously being sold abroad. And the prices of more expensive consumer goods such as TV sets, refrigerators and cars remained very high. Hundreds of thousands regularly spent their summer holidays on the Baltic or the Black Sea, or even further afield. The remarkable successes of GDR athletes in international contests, the wide-ranging chances of education at all levels for all young people (and many others) who were prepared to work hard, the general atmosphere of goodwill and mutual aid all contributed to a genuine "GDR-patriotism" among the majority of the younger generation. And millions of citizens (many more than the 2.3 million SED-members and candidates) were impressed by the general diplomatic recognition accorded the GDR in the early 1970s and its admission to the United Nations.

Economic difficulties.

At the same time the signs of economic difficulties and of unsolved problems were evident to everyone who kept his eyes open. A problem of enormous dimensions, never seriously tackled, remained that of labour discipline and productivity. In those branches of the economy which could not function at all without discipline, such as the railway, all seemed well. And where individual wages were based largely on the numbers or weight of products, productivity depended mainly on the quality of raw materials and on technical equipment. But where it was impossible to check or control the labour of each worker or employee, discipline deteriorated in degrees often difficult to believe. The worst example was probably the building industry. It was almost impossible to pass a building site without noticing that many workers were sitting around and that others were playing cards or coming and going, and that few or none were working. Buildings in the course of construction were never finished on time. If one asked for the reason, the answer was always the same: the materials required had not been delivered.

From 1976 to 1978 my wife could not but observe the slow progress of the erection of a five-storey block of flats nearby. The workers would always arrive on Monday afternoon having left their homes far from Berlin in the morning; they left on Thursday evening. No one worked on Fridays, let alone Saturdays. It took a year and a half to complete this simple, standard-type house.

In offices, except for the state administration, it became the general custom for female employees to do their daily shopping in working hours. In a place we knew, a large home for old-age pensioners, the nurses and secretaries even went to the hairdresser. It was the custom there to extend the coffee break at 9 a.m. until about 10 o'clock. Here, as in industry, it was difficult to do much against this sort of thing because of the acute scarcity of labour. If an employee was fired who was to replace him? At the entrance of virtually every factory or combine large placards stated which kind of workers were needed there, and appealed to those interested to report to the employment department.

This situation handicapped us even at the university. Secretaries who were able to do more than type and answer the telephone became rare in the 1970s, with the result that typists were often promoted to secretaries without being able to do that job properly. Clerical employees being badly paid, some faculties were left without any in the 1980s, and clerical work had to be done by younger scholars. At my sub-department, where there was only one secretary, who was often ill or temporarily requisitioned by the director, the members therefore had to spend quite a lot of time on work far below their academic qualification.

The shortage of labour was felt in many spheres, especially in those with low wages. Newsstands were usually open only from 7 to 10 p.m. because the women employed there would not work for any longer. In post offices with four or five counters often only one or two would be open – for the others there was no one to serve customers, with the result that queuing was frequent. Railway coaches on local or regional lines were frequently kept running for days before being cleaned; there were not enough cleaners. Public toilets were everywhere few and far between; no one would work as attendant.

It had in the 1960s become clear that the absence of foreign labour, which contributed so much to economic development in West Germany, Britain and France, was harming GDR economy substantially. When I raised the question with economists or government experts the answer was always the same: if we recruited labour abroad we had, on principle, to offer such workers the same conditions, especially housing, as our own had, and we were unable to do this. We could not possibly accommodate a dozen workers in one cellar, as was common in the West. The GDR could never maintain a sector of unskilled, underprivileged workers, considering how appalling the treatment of foreign labour in Germany had been even before 1933, let alone under Hitler. In the upshot there was some employment of Poles and Hungarians in various places, and of tens of thousands of Vietnamese in the textile industry in Saxony, but on the whole the contribution of foreign labour remained small.

A problem which was to become even more serious was the lack of foreign freely convertible currency. Because the GDR produced only a minor part of the raw materials its industry processed or of the products needed for other purposes such as petrol or anthracite, it had to import these. About three quarters were regularly obtained from the Soviet Union at very favourable prices, and from other socialist countries, but the remaining quarter had to be bought on the world market where prices since around 1970 catapulted to unheard of heights. Therefore exports to non-socialist countries had to be increased from year to year. The resulting strains on the economy had to be overcome by plunging the state into high debts. At the same time the means used to obtain western currency became more extreme all the time; political and other objections to the methods employed were disregarded, even when methods were dubious. (That political prisoners were actually sold to the Federal Republic for hard cash was an incredible affair kept secret in the GDR until its end. No one ever spoke about it in my presence and I do not think many of our people knew, since in the Federal Republic it appears to have been rarely touched upon publicly.)

At the university the shortage of western currency was increasingly felt and gradually reached serious proportions. In the 1960s we could count on being granted enough Deutschmarks or dollars to order the western literature we needed most for our work and to pay for travel to the countries whose history we were studying – providing the governments of these countries would admit us, which was often not the case. But in the 1970s the means available were drastically reduced and travel to Western Europe, Africa or Asia could only be financed in far fewer cases than before. If at all possible, academic exchange was made use of, but many younger scholars in our department were now seriously hampered by not even being able to take part in conferences abroad, let alone buy the books essential for their research. As the *Deutsche Staatsbibliothek* (state library) was also no longer getting western money and was reduced to the acquisition of western literature by exchanging GDR publications for whatever was thought most important, it could not fill the gap.

Some economists have written since 1990 that the economy of the GDR could not survive because fundamental structural defects condemned it to decline and eventual collapse. But were labour discipline and productivity, bad organisation, shortage of labour and shortage of western currency "structural defects"? Hardly. The basic weaknesses of our society were not economic.

African and Asian Studies.

My transfer to the Department of Asian (and African) Studies in 1971 turned out to be a change for the better. It had been founded only three years before by combining half-a-dozen small institutes and when I arrived it still breathed the optimism of a new foundation. The professors and lecturers were a friendly, professionally competent crowd. Most of them had only recently been appointed and there was only one older scholar of real distinction among them, the Egyptologist Fritz Hintze. They were too sensible to waste their time with frequent and long staff meetings, as had been the case in my former department.

As an older colleague with much professional experience and an anti-Nazi background, the scholars of the department treated me with respect. During my fifteen years there I never had trouble with any of them, with the sole exception of a rather temperamental lady member of my sub-department, whose opinions on how it should be run differed considerably from mine. But this was only a passing episode. Serious differences among the staff seldom arose. The only cases to cause bad blood concerned appointment to professional chairs: twice lecturers whose standing fully justified promotion were passed over in favour of others, seemingly for political reasons. But here prime responsibility rested with the Ministry of Higher Education. In one case I went to see a deputy minister, but to no avail. The candidate whose appointment I wanted to be postponed so that another could be promoted had three arguments in her favour: she was female, she was an SED member, and she had studied in the Soviet Union.

In his study, Spring 1984.
Photo: Andreas Trogisch

The number of students increased from year to year, but it remained smaller than in the large departments of the university. Therefore staff members could devote attention to each student and knew their students better than was possible at those departments. Among my students I only rarely discovered one not really interested in what I was teaching – a welcome difference to former years. The department was handicapped, however, by being housed in six different buildings situated at some distance to each other.

Naturally staff members observed closely what was happening in the country or region they specialised in, and correspondingly paid less attention to developments in the GDR or the Federal Republic. Some had studied in the Soviet Union; quite a few had lived in "their" country or at least visited it repeatedly, with the effect that their horizon was much broader than that of the general run of academics, whose possibilities of travel beyond eastern Europe remained limited. A healthy realism was dominant, not cramped by the resolutions of the last session of the Central Committee, as had been the case in my former department. Brezhnev's dictum that national liberation in the Third World would necessarily lead to socialism there was rejected in discussions. To publish a direct rebuttal would have been impossible, however. In the party organisation, to which most staff members belonged, discussion of political problems was fairly open and free. The fact that the university party committee took little notice of what happened in the department probably contributed to this openness.

I joined the sub-department of African Studies, which then consisted of five linguists and two specialists on African literature. I lectured there on African history and, for students from other departments, on colonial history from the 16th to the 20th century. From time to time I held seminars on historical methodology for PhD candidates. Three years later, in 1974, I was appointed head of the sub-department, a not very difficult or onerous position, since its members worked together in an almost unbelievable state of harmony and mutual aid, until, years later, stupid misbehaviour by a senior member spoiled the atmosphere for some time. It was also in 1974 that I finished work on the manuscript of a comprehensive history of German colonialism in Africa, as editor and main author. It aroused more interest than my previous publications; English and Russian translations were published in the following years.

In 1975 we celebrated the hundredth birthday of the founder of African studies at our university, Diedrich Westermann, and the fiftieth anni-

With a guest from Benin in the African Studies faculty, December 1974

versary of the chair for this discipline founded for him there. Westermann, originally a protestant missionary in Togo, had been a scholar of international standing and for years a co-director of the International Africa Institute in London. Our sub-department organised a conference, at which his work on African languages, ethnography and history as well as his attitude to the peoples of the continent were examined and critically assessed. This was not at all easy since Westermann had not only been a successful academic teacher and famous scholar, but had from his early years until the end of the Nazi regime actively supported German colonialism, even the preparations of that regime to restore German rule in Africa. But I think the eight speakers at our conference came near to a fair estimate of the merits, the limitations, and the in some respects unfathomable personality of our founder.

The conference confronted me, more than before, with the problem of our relations with the Department of African and Near Eastern studies of Leipzig University. During the preparations I learned to my surprise that this department had for some time also been preparing a conference on Westermann, with a similar agenda. Instead of joining

After the defence of the dissertation of A. A. Amr
(member of the Egyptian embassyin the GDR), May 1974.

forces with the Berlin africanists they had kept their preparations secret, evidently in the hope of stealing a march on us! Their curious behaviour had a background, of course.

African studies had hardly existed in Leipzig before 1960, when an African Institute was founded. Its inexperienced but ambitious first director regarded the Berlin institute of African Studies (our predecessor) as a serious danger to his prospects and tried hard to have it closed down, especially by describing it as the bulwark of reactionary colonialist traditions, which was, of course, nonsense, and by ridiculing its research projects, such as one on Togolese remnant languages, as irrelevant, which was harmful. His persistent campaign did not lead to the closing of the Berlin institute, but he succeeded in obtaining a ruling which limited it to only teaching students who took African studies as a second subject. While the Leipzig institute gradually grew, this director and his successor in the 1960s protested indignantly against the very idea of the Berlin institute being granted an additional assistant.

After the Department of African and Near Eastern Studies was founded in Leipzig in 1968 as an institution parallel to our Department at the Humboldt University its director Lothar Rathmann offered me a chair. When I declined and later took over the Berlin sub-department he was always outwardly friendly, but in practice his department continued the petty discrimination against our sub-department.

The idea of choosing another university than Berlin as *the* GDR centre for tackling the complicated field of African studies had been an unhappy one from the start; libraries in Berlin were far better and it was the seat of virtually all institutions with relations to African countries. The records of the former German Colonial Office, indispensable for historical research, were in the state archives in Potsdam near Berlin. The result of the mistaken choice of Leipzig was that many members of the Leipzig department spent half their time on trains between the two cities.

But these handicaps were not the main reason for the inadequate performance of the department in research during the twenty years of its existence. (Several of its members assured me that it was much better in teaching, which may be true.) The main reason was rather to be found in the policy pursued by Rathmann, by nature more a manager than a scholar, who laid greater stress on activities with an immediate but short-lived political effect than on long-term, scholarly work. His department held innumerable conferences but produced few books or articles which could be described as contributions to scientific advance. But when, at the celebration of its tenth anniversary, I said in my somewhat jocular congratulatory address that I had one wish for the department: fewer conferences and more sizeable books, some of the staff members present were offended.

After writing these lines I ask myself if I am not being unfair to my Leipzig colleagues. The department there consisted of three sub-departments: one dealt with basic problems, one with sub-Saharan Africa, and one with the Near East and North Africa. I cannot comment on the last mentioned, since my contacts with it were few and far between. Its only important publication, a history of the Arab peoples in seven volumes, is regarded by specialists as valuable in parts. It was translated into Arabic and distributed widely in the Near East.

The other two sub-departments had among their staff members some excellent scholars and devoted socialists, who did useful work on African economy, constitutions, political affairs, on notable German Africanists of the past such as Westermann and Frobenius, and other subjects. But they were obviously hampered by conditions imposed by Rathmann, who had the full support of the Department of Sciences of the Central Committee. As for the second sub-department, the economist Gerda Weinberger wrote interesting articles on South Africa which regularly provoked controversy. But the only book worth mentioning which the sub-department produced on African history was an outline of pre-colonial times, which was not without its weaknesses, but certainly useful. It was the first volume of a four-volume history of sub-Saharan Africa. The other three volumes were uneven in quality, the second on Africa from 1884 till 1945 being disgracefully bad. The third and the fourth were handbooks, not historical narratives but products of political science. Some of the professors of this department were so untalented that they would never have been appointed at the Humboldt University. On my journeys home from the conferences I was obliged to attend in Leipzig I usually felt depressed or angry.

The absolute zero level among the conferences was reached by the largest, an international assembly on the hundredth anniversary of the Berlin Conference on the Partition of Africa of 1884-5. I had begun consultations in 1982 about the project of an international conference in Berlin on the history of colonialism in Africa on this occasion with the participation of as many African historians as possible. Such a conference could well have been an important contribution to greater clarity about the modern history of the "black continent", which had been obscured beyond all measure by apologists of colonial rule. Such a conference would undoubtedly have served African interests, met African expectations, and enhanced the prestige of the GDR in Africa.

But Rathmann and people influenced by him in the staff of the Central Committee decided that the anniversary should serve as occasion for a conference on "Colonialism, Neo-colonialism and Africa's Path to a Peaceful Future", i.e. on any and all African problems. 350 scholars, writers and politicians from 31 countries took part in this assembly; more than 100 papers were presented on political, ideological, economic, and historical subjects. I do not know how much the conference cost, but its contribution to historical writing on Africa, as reflected in subsequent publications, was nil. Since no papers in full but only short summaries of papers were published in English, this result did not surprise me. The conference was apparently forgotten after a few months, which cannot be said of the international symposium of historians on the occasion of the same anniversary which took place in West Berlin at the same time.

Laudable in principle was the publication of articles and conference papers in English translation in paperbacks by the Leipzig department. But the translations were often painfully bad. I never heard of any of these paperbacks being quoted in Africa or anywhere else. Their distribution seems to have been quite inadequate. The books of the French Marxist Jean Suret-Canale on African history were to be found in many African bookshops; the Leipzig publications were not.

It is now clearer to me than at the time that the numerous faults and weaknesses, of which I have mentioned only a part, were possible only because of the faulty development of the SED in the 1970s and 1980s. Standards of socialist morality and demands on the character and behaviour of party members had declined since the 1960s, as I have already described. Only under the conditions now prevailing was it possible in Leipzig for somebody to become a professor who kept a card index at his home with files of persons he met or worked with, in which he recorded their utterances in order to use them against these persons in future if he should find it expedient. (This curious activity had – as far as I know – no connection with the state secret service.) Another of the Leipzig professors was an ill-tempered petty tyrant who tended to push his subordinates around. Such people would not have been tolerated as professors at the Gewifa when I was a student. But, I repeat, other Leipzig colleagues were decent, sincere, good characters. Their university could be proud to have such brilliant scholars as Walter Markov, his pupil Manfred Kossok, and the medieval historian Ernst Werner among its teachers.

With Apollon B. Davidson (Moscow) in Berlin, Summer 1980.

A most welcome compensation for my experiences with Leipzig were the really fruitful and increasingly friendly relations I established with colleagues in Moscow. Apollon Davidson and his assistants and pupils at the Academy of Sciences of the USSR and Moscow University were splendid partners. Here I was welcomed without ill-concealed fear of any criticism and invited to take part in their work, which I gladly did whenever possible. After they had come to know me well they spoke to me quite openly about their own problems and weaknesses. They helped me whenever they could, and I helped them. To this day I feel grateful for their true and unselfish friendship. It turned out that Moscow knew the same dichotomy between serious scholarship and thin political rodomontade as Leipzig. But among historians of Africa the first was dominant.

In the late 1960s I became interested in South Africa, read more litera-ture of all kinds about it and made friends with South African exiles. When visiting London for research on apartheid, my host was repeat-edly the well known ANC-official M. P. Naicker, at that time head of ANC propaganda and editor of its monthly *Sechaba*, who introduced me to many other ANC exiles. Their situation was not dissimilar to that of German and other exiles in England many years before. As the very popular "M. P.", as he was generally known, told me, former anti-Nazi resistance fighters in the GDR had taught them methods of

*At a meeting of the UN Anti-Apartheid Special Committee in Berlin with
G. Silundika, Secretary of Information of the ZAPU (Zimbabwe), May 1974*

smuggling people and illegal literature across borders and distributing
them. All of them were very grateful to our country for the considerable political, material and educational support they had received from
it for years.

The history of South Africa in general and the apartheid system in particular became a main field of activity for me in the 1970s and early
1980s. I lectured on it before many audiences, wrote articles and
papers, and organised conferences dealing with apartheid. Large conferences on this subject were held at our university in 1976 and 1981.
Some of the opinions aired there may have been wide of the mark, but
they helped to make people aware of the necessity of putting an end to
the criminal system under which the African population of South
Africa was suffering, and thus served an extremely good cause.

There were few fields in which GDR policy, in contrast to the policy of
the western powers, was finally supported so unreservedly by a large
part of our people. For me, the South African question was no unpoli-
tical niche, into which I had fled to escape GDR realities, but it did to
some extent divert my attention from internal defects.

School education.

In the 1970s, after we had moved to East Berlin, we were confronted with our educational system from the viewpoint of parents. In Kleinmachnow we had been satisfied with the school our boys went to after completing three years at the kindergarten, which had systematically prepared them for what was to come. Our elder boy's form had been in the hands of a really excellent woman teacher trained for primary education (i.e. the first four years, for 6- to 10-year olds), whom we liked from the first parents' meeting and came to know quite well after she had visited us, as was customary when children began school. The school was in a suitable building, equipped with modern educational aids and instruments of all kinds, and the children seemed happy enough. The atmosphere pointed to carefully guided activities for the children. The only problem we became aware of was that there were hardly any male teachers; education seemed to have become an almost exclusively female vocation, which could hardly be ideal for boys. And teachers complained of being burdened with too many tasks outside the school, such as visiting parents and helping at elections.

In Berlin things were very different. The school was situated in an old, dismal building, as forbidding as the official architecture in imperial Germany before 1918 could be. The teachers were a cheerless lot, well-meaning but helpless, clinging to instructions from above, many of them incapable of maintaining discipline, which as a result was bad throughout the school. The headmaster who relied on personal connections with people in the local administration to keep him in his job, while not making any attempt to improve an insupportable situation. The only teacher on whom we had placed some hopes left the school for a position in a manufacturing works some months after our boys entered it. The hopelessly incapable female teacher of Russian who was in charge of our younger son's form was not removed although the parents' meetings for that form which we regularly attended kept on demanding that she be replaced. Under these circumstances we had to keep a careful eye on our boys' progress at school and frequently helped them, so that after the 8th form when they had reached the age of 14 their results were good enough for transfer to a secondary school.

It should be said here that discipline in schools was generally known to be bad in the larger cities, especially in their more densely populated districts. It was not improved by the strict rule that teachers, who were held personally responsible for their pupils' progress, should pay the most attention to the weakest pupils and at all costs prevent their having to repeat a year's schooling. Since the teachers themselves had to assess their pupils' progress and teachers, like other people, as a rule did not like admitting failure, even the weakest were usually dragged along with the best. The latter, who easily fulfilled the tasks set, were often left to themselves by the teachers and became used to spending their time on something of their own choosing. The result, of course, was that teaching as a whole suffered. The better pupils learned less than they could have done and talents were often not developed.

A case in point was Russian. Its introduction into the curriculum of every elementary school from the 5th year onwards was, theoretically, a great step forward: who had ever heard of a foreign language being taught to the children of working men, low grade employees, or peasants? But the results of four, later six, years of teaching were, in most schools, nil or extremely poor, often a sheer mockery. The reasons for this were manifold. The teachers of Russian were usually very young and inexperienced, and the least able to uphold discipline. A high proportion of parents did not see why their children should learn such a difficult language, with a very strange alphabet which constituted a psychological barrier. Last but not least, hardly any boy or girl was ever refused a certificate of successful completion of school after 8 (later 10) years because of insufficient knowledge of Russian.

Parents known to be interested in the school were usually expected to help when difficulties arose which the teachers could not succeed in coping with. When a boy in our younger son's class repeatedly failed to turn up for school and the teacher responsible for him could not get in touch with his unmarried mother – he was an illegitimate child – three of us who were not working that morning went to see her. The woman, who made a slovenly impression, worked in a restaurant as a wardrobe attendant. She explained that she was unable to control the boy and could not stop him missing lessons. We appealed to her to fulfil her duties as a mother and tried to impress on her that the boy would not be accepted anywhere for an apprenticeship without completing at least nine years at school, knowing that, even if she took our visit seriously, there was little chance of change. Cases of this kind were not rare in the big cities. The local authority, informed by the school, would delegate a member of its social welfare department to see what could be done. (There were never truant officers in Germany.) Of course it could have had the mother hauled before court if this went on for any length of time, but under the circumstances the court would simply have admonished and not punished her.

We left the mother in a depressed state of mind. The visit, short as it was, had demonstrated vividly that twenty years after the construction of socialism had been proclaimed, parts of the working class in the big cities still lived under conditions which, by German standards, could only be described as ranging from bad to appalling. Of course unemployment had disappeared long ago – except for those who disliked work and maintained an existence of sorts financed by the local authority – violent crime was almost unknown, and prostitution was limited to a few places frequented by visitors from western countries. Habitual criminals had virtually all emigrated westwards; there were neither tramps nor beggars. But there was still a minority, mainly of unskilled labourers, unable or unwilling to provide their children with conditions under which they could rise above the poverty, and often drunkenness and squalor of their parents.

The secondary school our boys attended after completing the 8th form of the elementary school (its official status was *Erweiterte Oberschule*), one of 14 of its type in East Berlin, bore the name of the famous artist Käthe Kollwitz, who had lived in our district. It was much better than the elementary school, but I sometimes asked myself if she would have liked it. Probably not. After some years' acquaintance with it I concluded with much regret that in important respects it did not reach the standards of the grammar school where I had been a pupil in England in the 1930s. In mathematics and natural sciences demands on the pupils were much higher than I had experienced, but in other subjects, such as geography, history, foreign languages, this was not the case. Most of the teachers had originally taught at elementary schools and been transferred to secondary schools with no or little additional training; very few of them pursued scholarly interests or hobbies. The books the pupils had to use were very good indeed, but the teachers did not always stick to them and control was often superficial.

There was no character building or attempt to instil respect for the teachers. Our elder boy's class master, a spineless type, kept on telling his pupils that he would not be teaching if he were clever enough for a better profession. An esprit de corps or pride in the school were also lacking. At my grammar school in England these had been promoted by school blazers and caps and was part of a middle class outlook, which could occasionally be seen in condescending or contemptuous remarks about the "lower orders" or even "the great unwashed" by some boys. When I asked the headmaster of the Käthe-Kollwitz-School whether it would not be a good idea to inculcate pride in the pupils and teachers in their socialist school he replied that the Ministry of

Education (headed by Honecker's wife) would regard any move in such a direction as an attempt to restore the old, bourgeois German *Gymnasium* (secondary school), which had been abolished years before.

The strong egalitarian principles which were dominant in GDR education in the fifties and sixties were now however, under the pressure of constant criticism by scientists and other people of influence, being gradually pushed back. Specialized schools for youngsters gifted in this or that direction were founded for sports, Russian, mathematics etc. Additionally, at a few universities so called "pupils' societies" under the guidance of a lecturer were founded for mathematics. Money was always forthcoming to promote sports (including chess) among school children and other young people.

But the Ministry of Education under Margot Honecker and the regional and district administrations usually remained impervious to criticism from any quarters except those on high. There was virtually no discussion of school problems in the newspapers – publications on educational matters had, without exception, to vetted by the educational authorities. Letters of complaint on educational subjects I sent to newspapers and journals were never published. In the seventies there was, among university teachers, widespread resignation on this subject. When Honecker became first secretary of the party in 1971 the head of our institute said to me: "Oh my god! Now we won't get rid of that minister of education (Honecker's wife) for ages." Unfortunately he was right, though I am not sure if another minister would have changed much. There was a whole camarilla of educationalists in office who clung obstinately to their ideas, injurious as these were to the whole of our society and, being a state within the state, would not budge, since they could be sure of the necessary support in the Politburo.

Their very strong position was, when closely examined, astounding, for it was not difficult to see that the educational system had serious weaknesses. Since the sixties myriads of young people were taught the virtues of peace, of friendship among all people, of human progress and solidarity. It was almost impossible to detect among them any vestiges of nationalism, racism, contempt for parts of our society other than their own. Confidence in human progress was widespread. But, as far as human society was concerned, they were taught a simplified Marxist theory reduced to dogma. Many of those who taught it were unable to bring it into a coherent and convincing relationship with historical and social realities. How could the GDR be progressive and the Federal Republic be reactionary if the latter had better cars, superior fashions, greater freedom of travel? How could the Soviet Union be more progressive than the United States, considering that the latter had a much higher standard of living? There was no open discussion of such problems in the schools, which would have been more important than well-founded explanations of the origins and character of both world wars.

German history, as taught in the schools, was certainly closer to realities than the corresponding teaching in the Federal Republic. But history teaching in general all too often centred on the (simplified) explanation of theoretical concepts such as feudalism, absolutism, capitalism, imperialism. This could, of course, be no substitute the teaching of real, live, colourful, often dramatic and infinitely manifold human development.

In spite their outer uniformity, secondary schools remained different from each other as far as the standards of teaching was concerned. Judging by what I heard from colleagues, not all of them had the faults of the Käthe-Kollwitz-School. But since the final school examinations were carried out by the teachers themselves and not by boards interested in objective evaluation, the examination results were not a reliable basis for decisions on admission to universities. Many university departments therefore conducted their own (unofficial) entrance examinations.

Another general weakness of the school system consisted in the high turnover of teachers. All too many young people who had trained for the teaching profession left it after a few years to work in other fields. When dealing with editorial offices of all kinds, libraries, publishers, museums, cultural or scientific bodies, many of the people I met had one characteristic in common: they had received four years' training as teachers.

Socialism disfigured.

An institution which, as has only become clear since 1989, played a very important part in disfiguring socialism in the GDR in the 1970s and 1980s was the internal department of the Ministry of State Security (*Staatssicherheitsdienst* or *Stasi*). I have not mentioned it so far because I had no connection with it and did not realise how important it was until after the GDR had collapsed. It was no Gestapo, which after all murdered hundreds of thousands of its prisoners. But it did on occasion ill treat people badly and employed methods which can only be described as infamous.

What else is the practice of instructing lawyers, who secretly belonged to it, to take on the defence of young people accused of calumny of the state, so that these lawyers would be able to hand on to State Security the confidential information they might obtain from the accused? At the time none of us would have believed this. But obviously the heads of the service thought that the ends justified any means, and that in matters of State Security there was no such thing as socialist morality. We would also not have believed that Honecker, Mielke and their associates would ever, even if only within limits, support West German terrorists, who were trying to bring down capitalism by murder. But the capital sin of Honecker was not these cases of complete lack of scruples, but the policy – which somehow agreed with such cases – of basing security less and less on the convinced support of the people and increasingly on an apparatus which expanded more and more and whose members became an isolated and unpopular body. Because of their extensive privileges they were in the 1980s a state within the state. At my successive departments at the university the *Stasi* was never spoken of. There may well have been students who did not even know such an institution existed. My own experience with them was insignificant. They only twice tried to recruit me. One day, I think it was 1960, a quiet little man came to the department of history to question some of the party members there about Gerda Grothe, the lecturer from West Berlin. The questions gave me the impression that he was gathering information as an agent in her part of the city. I told him that I thought that she was a brilliant scholar with strong ties to our university. She had some sympathies for the GDR but no strong ties. (This answer could do her no harm.)

He then asked if I would not prepared to join the *Stasi* as an unofficial informer, to which I replied that I would not since I was going to be promoted to a professorship and this status was not compatible with that kind of work. He accepted my answer, struck my name off a list lying in front of him and ended our conversation.

The second attempt took place years later, about 1978. One afternoon three men turned up at our flat – I was alone – and introduced themselves as members of the *Stasi*. The youngest, about 24 years of age, seemed to be a trainee, since the elder, more than twice his age, treated him as a pupil. The third, a man of about 35, asked me various questions about my work and about the political situation in Africa, about which he knew little. Then he spoke about the advantages I would enjoy if I joined them, above all I would be able to travel freely to West Germany. When I replied that I was not interested, since that country had almost nothing to offer for my work, he was astonished. After some more talk about Africa they left. The truth was that I had decided in the 1950s never to do secret service work if I could avoid it. As a member of such a service I would no longer be my own master but compelled to carry out the orders of my superiors, however distasteful these might be. I did not need the *Stasi's* money and was not certain that I would be able to stand up to pressure if arrested abroad.

At party elections I was never put forward as a candidate; therefore my party work was limited to occasional remarks and meetings, usually on foreign affairs. In the 1970s I became gradually aware of discontent among some members of our faculty. Not that they opposed socialism or supported western policies. Socialism continued to be axiomatic; if anyone at the university doubted its inherent superiority he or she was careful not to say so.

But there was very little genuine political discussion. For the annual election meeting of the party the candidates were carefully selected beforehand and had to be approved by the university party committee, although the elections were secret. Within the SED, the process of decision making evolved in such a way that more the more important a decision, the smaller the influence of party members.

At this point the reader may well asked what the position of the author to the GDR and the SED in the 1970s and 1980s was, seeing how much he had to criticize. The answer is not simple. Much as there was to criticize, condemn or reject I always remained fully aware of the importance of upholding such a bastion of peace and aid for anti-colonial progress in Central Europe. Like millions of other GDR citizens I did not want to see the GDR weakened, let alone destroyed. With all its faults it continued to be a real bulwark of peace in Europe. Even in the 1980s there was much "GDR Patriotism" and not a little justified pride in its achievements.

But for a considerable part of our people the Federal Republic continued to be an object of great interest or envy. Materially it had so much more to offer: cars at prices which nearly everyone could afford, travel to very many countries (provided the traveller could pay), and many many other advantages. It was usually forgotten that the Federal Republic had the highest standard of living in non-socialist Europe. The other Germany, and not Portugal or Greece, was "the West".

The leaders of the GDR must have observed this development with increasing apprehension. A number of advisers advocated reforming the entire economic structure. But the GDR economy was too closely tied to the economy of the Soviet Union for far-reaching changes to be carried out without the assent and cooperation of the giant on whose support it had always depended. And Brezhnev, conservative to the bone and unwilling to take risks, strictly rejected basic reforms, evidently fearing that they would endanger the "socialist" system in the Soviet Union. We now know that in the early 1970s relations between Honecker and his associates and the Soviet leadership were strained. This does not appear to have lasted long and remained unknown to our people (including me). Industry in the GDR to a very large extent depended on Soviet imports and there may well have been no other possibility than to give way and continue practicing, basically, the existing system, which was from time to time the subject of helpless attempts at improvement.

In order to alleviate the discontent about the scarcity and poor quality of many sorts of consumer goods, hundreds and later thousands of *intershops* were opened, where for Western currency (whose possession was prohibited by law!) one could buy goods of Western manufacture at high prices. In the 1980s these shops became an important source of foreign currency for the government. The population was thus split into two parts. A fairly large part could buy Western goods with the money sent them by relations in the Federal Republic, the other part could not. A more serious result was that young people, who streamed into these shops in huge numbers simply to gape at the commodities offered for sale, were deeply impressed and concluded that Western goods were far superior to ours.

These changes were evident to everyone. Not evident to our people, except for a small minority, were a number of other measures intended to stabilise the GDR or increase its standing in the eyes of the world. These measures were extremely dishonest or disreputable. Although my family, my colleagues and I knew nothing about them – they became generally known only after 1990 – I have to say something about them, because they played an important part in enabling the GDR to survive longer. Without its dishonesty the Honecker regime could certainly not have existed until late 1989.

Of great political importance were the successes in international sports. The state spent much money for the necessary facilities over the years and "socialist sport" became an integral part of the life of our youth. Since there was no commercial sport – being amateurs, top ranking athletes only occasionally received financial rewards – this policy contributed a little to health, to moral standards and "socialist consciousness". But it has now become clear that successes in international contests were often due to the use of banned drugs by athletes.

This was obviously incompatible with the standard publicly demanded by the GDR sports authorities. The use of drugs had been officially condemned on many occasions when cases from Western teams were condemned as floating up from the capitalist cesspool. This was sheer hypocrisy on the part of the government.

For years before 1989 election results at all levels were falsified: the number of votes for the "National Front" officially published was higher that the actual number of these votes. The false figures published were fabricated at the highest level. Probably none of these falsifications showed so clearly the level of cretinism to which some of the leaders had sunk: the true figures were in very many cases quite high enough to give the "National Front" a comfortable majority, 80 or 90 per cent. But no, it had to be 98 per cent. And among the many hundreds of officials in charge of these infantile deceptions not a single one, as far as it is known, tried to break out of the cage of "party discipline" by refusing to carry them out.

The GDR was not condemned to end like this. But it would have needed a far-reaching transformation to reach a socialism worthy of its name.

Socialism emasculated

The ignominious collapse of socialism in the Soviet Union and other countries of Eastern and Central Europe was not a collapse of socialism absolutely and for all time. Rather, it seems to have been the collapse of a specific model of socialism (in the GDR and Czechoslovakia perhaps less so than elsewhere) which increasingly proved incapable of fulfilling important claims made for it such as its democratic nature and human rights. It finally degenerated to a system of deception and material corruption.

Not wishing to admit the full truth about the economic situation, the GDR government published distorted or false statistics. A favoured method since 1973 was the publication of percentages instead of absolute figures. Some years later, an expert from the state economic commission, lectured at a party meeting I went to. When, at the end, I asked why so many statistics were published which gave no clear picture, the answer was: "But comrade, have you no confidence in our leaders?" This reply was characteristic, as was the fact that it was accepted without open protest by the meeting. In the course of the 1970s the membership of the SED had become accustomed never to question the unfailing wisdom of its superiors.

In the 1980s at least a dozen political leaders misappropriated public funds to have private residences built, or hunting grounds maintained. In one case I was told about a member of the Central Committee who had bought grounds on the shore of a well-known lake near Berlin from the local authority – an absolutely illegal proceeding, since the land sold was part of a nature reserve area.

This sort of thing was, of course, kept secret though nonetheless in the early eighties it was virtually impossible to travel by taxi in East Berlin without being told about it by the driver. The number of people who clearly offended socialist morality remained tiny, but none of my colleagues or I ever heard of Honecker or the Politburo taking action against it.

Inevitably the violation of socialist principles by leaders would have badly harmed their authority, if it became known. But it remained almost secret; stories of this kind were in the party dismissed as western propaganda. Democratic practice in our society was quite a different matter, of course. At a meeting of our trade union branch in the late 1970s a non-party member once said: "The party and state leaders rule us like benevolent despots." This was fairly near the truth and no one objected. At the same time the "party worker" was increasingly replaced by a person who was, in essence, an official.

In the 1970s the socialist standards and values which had distinguished our life so clearly from that of people in West Germany gradually receded into the background. Odd as it may seem, I observed more than once that the superiority of the "western way of life" was impressively demonstrated in exhibitions, trade shows etc. After 1973 there was no longer any serious opposition in leading circles to watching West German TV, which became a habit for the majority of GDR viewers and exerted much influence, being technically superior to ours. Among younger people socialist habits were often replaced by a "Honecker socialism", based on concessions to the "western way of life". The entrances of many flats and summer-houses could now well have had the motto attached "You are leaving the socialist sphere of influence".

During my last years at the university I had little contact with young people, having only a few students, and spending much time on research. But it was impossible not to notice that they were, as a whole, nowhere near an attitude which would enable them to successfully continue the work of the generation which built the GDR.

Young people were carefully guided, looked after and protected against all possible dangers to such an extent that their capacity to think independently and critically, fend for themselves and stand up not only to their parents but to the world in general was distinctly underdeveloped. It was here that the most important internal reason for the final collapse of the GDR lay. How could youth wholeheartedly support, let alone fight for, a society whose government openly distrusted them by not letting them visit western countries? And by not giving them free access to western printed publications which need not have included the gutter press? And not offered them instead the tawdry substitutes of "Honecker socialism"? Levi's jeans could well have been done without if there had been government by the people and the conviction that socialism offered a genuine and better alternative.

1974

List of selected publications

I. Books

Deutschland und China im 19. Jahrhundert. Das Eindringen des deutschen Kapitalismus, Berlin 1958 (Chinese translation: Peking 1961)

Kamerun unter deutscher Kolonialherrschaft. Studien, Bd. 1, Berlin 1960; Bd. 2, Berlin 1968 (editor)

Handbuch der Verträge 1871-1964, Berlin 1968 (editor, with Adolf Rüger)

Biographisches Lexikon zur deutschen Geschichte. Von den Anfängen bis 1945, Berlin 1967, 2nd edition 1970 (co-editor)

Walter Stoecker. Die Frühzeit eines deutschen Arbeiterführers 1891-1920, Berlin 1970

Drang nach Afrika. Die koloniale Expansionspolitik und Herrschaft des deutschen Kapitalismus in Afrika von den Anfängen bis zum Ende des zweiten Weltkrieges, Berlin 1977 (editor), 2nd revised edition 1991; Russian translation: Istoria germanskogo kolonializma w Afrike, Moskau 1983; English translation: German Imperialism in Africa, London 1986

Rassendiskriminierung, Kolonialpolitik und ethnisch-nationale Identität. Referate des 2. Internationalen Kolonialgeschichtlichen Symposiums 1991 in Berlin, Münster/Hamburg 1992 (co-editor)

II. Articles

Zur Politik Bismarcks in der englisch-russischen Krise von 1885, in: Zeitschrift für Geschichtswissenschaft (ZfG), Berlin 1956, S. 1187-1202

Der Eintritt Preussens und Deutschlands in die Reihe der in China bevorrechteten Mächte, in: ZfG, 1957, S. 603-606

Die deutsche Annexion von Kamerun 1884, in: Wissenschaftliche Zeitschrift der Karl-Marx-Universität Leipzig. Gesellschafts- und sprachwissenschaftliche Reihe, 1958/59, H. 4

Die deutsche Geschichtsschreibung der Gegenwart über die imperialistische Kolonialpolitik, in: Wissenschaftliche Zeitschrift der Humboldt-Universität zu Berlin. Gesellschafts- und sprachwissenschaftliche Reihe, 1959/60, H. 1/2 ·

Die Vorschläge der Sowjetunion für allgemeine und vollständige Abrüstung 1927/28, in: ZfG, 1961, S. 13-27 (with G. Rosenfeld)

Zur Politik der Westmächte im August und September 1939, in: Der deutsche Imperialismus und der Zweite Weltkrieg, vol. 2, Berlin 1961

Bemerkungen über die deutschen Kriegsziele in Afrika südlich der Sahara, in: Wissenschaftliche Zeitschrift der Humboldt-Universität zu Berlin, Gesellschafts- und sprachwissenschaftliche Reihe, 1964, H. 7

Vorbemerkung, in: Der deutsche Faschismus in Lateinamerika 1933-1943, Berlin 1966 (editorship)

The Expansionist Policy of Imperialist Germany in Africa South of the Sahara 1908 – 1918, in: Études africaines/African Studies/Afrika-Studien, Leipzig 1967

Forschungen zur Geschichte Afrikas (with W. Markov and H. Nimschowski), in: Historische Forschungen in der DDR 1960-1970. Analysen und Berichte. ZfG-Sonderband zum XIII. Internationalen Historikerkongreß in Moskau 1970, Berlin 1970

Das Eindringen des deutschen Kapitalismus in China im 19. Jahrhundert, in: Asien in Vergangenheit und Gegenwart, in: Beiträge der Asienwissenschaftler der DDR zum XXIX. Internationalen Orientalistenkongreß 1973 in Paris, Berlin 1974

Ein exponierter Vorposten der Apartheid. Zur Lage des Rassistenregimes in Südrhodesien (Simbabwe), in: asien-afrika-lateinamerika (aala), 1975, H. 1

Bürgerliche Auslegungen des Imperialismusbegriffes in der Gegenwart, in: Studien zum deutschen Imperialismus vor 1914, ed. by F. Klein, Berlin 1976

Das Verhältnis von Rassismus und Imperialismus unter besonderer Berücksichtigung des südlichen Afrika, in: aala, 1976, S. 751-758

Diedrich Westermanns ideologische Stellung und seine Haltung gegenüber den Völkern Afrikas, in: Wissenschaftliche Zeitschrift der Humboldt-Universität zu Berlin, Gesellschafts- und sprachwissenschaftliche Reihe, 1976, H. 2

Preußisch-deutsche Chinapolitik in den 1860/70er Jahren, in: H.-U. Wehler (ed.): Imperialismus, Köln 1976

The transition to the Colour Bar in British West Africa, in: aala, special issue 2, 1977

Germany and China 1861-94, in: J.A. Moses/P. Kennedy (eds.): Germany in the Pacific and Far East, 1870-1914, New York etc. 1977

An African Bourgeoisie in South Africa?, in: Social Classes and anti-imperialist struggle in Africa and the Middle East, Berlin 1978

The development of Geman colonies in Africa. Some observations on trends and consequences, in: African Studies/Afrika-Studien. Dedicated to the IVth International Congress of Africanists in Kinshasa, Berlin 1978

Recent Anglo-South African Liberal Historiography on the African Peoples of South Africa, in: L. Krizsán (ed.): Sources and Historiography on African Liberation Movements. Studies on Developing Countries no. 96, Budapest 1978

Die Rolle der Historiographie im Kampf um Südafrika, in: aala, 1979, H. 6

Arbeiterbewegung und Kolonialfrage. Die deutsche Sozialdemokratie und der antikoloniale Aufstand in Südwestafrika 1904-1907, in: XVe Congrès International des Sciences Historiques, Rapports II. Section Chronologique, Bukarest 1980

Probleme des Kampfes gegen Kolonialismus und Rassismus im Süden Afrikas, in: aala, 1980, H. 1

Forschungen zur Geschichte des subsaharischen Afrika (with Th. Büttner), in: Historische Forschungen in der DDR 1970-1980. Analysen und Berichte. ZfG-Sonderband zum XV. Internationalen Historiker-kongreß in Bukarest 1980, Berlin 1980

Apartheid and Colonialism: a comment, in: aala, special issue 6, 1980

Lesotho: Geschichte und Gegenwart, in: aala, 1981, H. 5

Some comments on ethnic processes and the problem of the nation in South Africa, in: Current problems of the Southern African Region, ed. by G. Brehme/G. Weinberger, Leipzig 1981

The Berlin Conference on the partition of Africa 1884-1885: some observations, in: Gerhard Brehme/Thea Büttner: African Studies – Afrika-Studien. Dedicated to the Vth Internatinal Congress of African Studies in Nigeria, Berlin 1983

Colonialism in Africa and Historical Progress, in: aala, special issue 13, 1984

Die Berliner Konferenz von 1884/85 über die koloniale Aufteilung Afrikas südlich der Sahara, in: aala, 1984, H. 5

Žapadnaja Afrika pod germanskim gospodstgrom, in: Istorija Afriki w XIX – načale XX w., Moskau 1984

Diedrich Westermann's Historical Views and Attitudes to African People (in Russian), in: Izuschenie istorii Afrikii. Problemij i dostischenija, Moskva 1985

Enemies of the Colonial Idea (with Peter Sebald); The Position of Africans in the German Colonies, both in: A.J. Knoll/L.H. Gann (eds.): Germans in the Tropics. Essays in German Colonial History, New York/Westport, Connecticut/London 1987

Die spezifischen Attribute der deutschen Kolonialherrschaft in Afrika. Zu einigen Auffassungen in der neueren Literatur, in: H. Christmann (ed.): Kolonisation und Dekolonisation. Referate des Internationalen Kolonialgeschichtlichen Symposiums '89 an der Pädagogischen Hochschule Schwäbisch-Gmünd, Schwäbisch-Gmünd 1989

Ein ungelöstes Problem südafrikanischer Geschichte. Die Ursprünge des Kriegerkönigtums der Zulu, in: ZfG, 1990, H. 8

Koloniale Rassendiskriminierung: Das Beispiel Britisch-Westafrika, in: W. Wagner et al. (eds.): Rassendiskriminierung, Kolonialpolitik und ethnisch-nationale Identität, Münster/Hamburg 1992

Germanophilie und Hoffnung auf Hitler in Togo und Kamerun zwischen den Weltkriegen, in: Peter Heine/Ulrich van der Heyden (eds.): Studien zur Geschichte des deutschen Kolonialismus in Afrika. Festschrift zum 60. Geburtstag von Peter Sebald, Pfaffenweiler 1995

Wie ich die Gründung erlebte; Die Internationale Jugendkonferenz 1942, both in: Das war unser Leben. Erinnerungen und Dokumente zur Geschichte der Freien Deutschen Jugend in Großbritannien 1939 – 1946, ed. by Alfred Fleischhacker, Berlin 1996

Biographical data

Helmuth Stoecker, born in 1920, was the first son of Walter Stoecker, a journalist and leading member of the German Communist Party. After his father's arrest by the Nazis immediately after the Reichstag Fire in February 1933, Helmuth and his younger sister had to emigrate to Britain. He was among the young German émigrés who founded the Free German Youth in Great Britain in 1939. In the same year he begun to study at the university of Bristol. In 1947 he returned to the Soviet zone of Germany and continued his studies in history, philosophy and economics at the universities at Leipzig and Berlin. He obtained his degree of doctor of philosophy in 1956 with a study on the colonial relations between Germany and China in the 19th century. In 1963 he completed postdoctoral work with a political biography of Walter Stoecker. Since 1957 he taught as a university lecturer, and in 1964 he became professor of modern history at the Humboldt University in Berlin. From 1974 to 1983 he was head of the Department of African Studies. In addition, he was a member of the Central Council of Asian, African, and Latin American Sciences in the German Democratic Republic and of the Advisory Council for Regional Studies at the Ministry of Higher Education. In 1986 he became professor emeritus. Helmuth Stoecker died in 1994 in Berlin.

Anpassung – Selbstbehauptung – Widerstand

Mirjam Michaelis
Die große und die kleine Welt
Herausgegeben und mit einem Nachwort
versehen von Irmgard Klönne, in Verbindung
mit Gabi Rochell und Renate Schiller-
Thielmann
Bd. 7, 1995, 144 S., 28,80 DM, br., ISBN 3-8258-2451-9

Simone Ladwig-Winters
**Wertheim – ein Warenhausunternehmen
und seine Eigentümer**
Ein Beispiel der Entwicklung der Berliner
Warenhäuser bis zur "Arisierung"
Während der Zeit des Nationalsozialismus ver-
loren die Eigentümer Hermann Tietz und Georg
Wertheim die Verfügungsgewalt über ihre Waren-
hausunternehmen.
Man weiß heute, *daß* das so war, Unklarheit
herrscht jedoch über das Wie. Die vorliegende
Arbeit nun schließt diese Lücke.
Am Beispiel Wertheim und H. Tietz wird gezeigt,
wie sich die Durchführung der Rassengesetze
erst auf Umsatz und Angebot der Warenhäuser
auswirkte und schließlich dazu führte, daß die
Eigentümer ihre Unternehmen verloren. Es wird
ein umfassendes Bild über die Entwicklung der
Berliner Warenhäuser bis zur Arisierung geschaf-
fen.
Bd. 8, 1997, 493 S., 68,80 DM, br., ISBN 3-8258-3062-4

Claus Cursiefen
Auf den Spuren Janusz Korczaks in Israel
Der polnisch-jüdische Kinderarzt, Schriftsteller
und Pädagoge Janusz Korczak bereiste in den 30er
Jahren zweimal das heutige Israel. Wie die beiden
Reisen 1934 und 1936 abliefen, wie sie Korczaks
persönliche Entwicklung und sein schriftstelleri-
sches Werk beeinflußten und welche Spuren sie
im heutigen Israel hinterließen, wurde im Rahmen
einer Studienreise untersucht.
Bd. 9, 1997, 48 S., 19,80 DM, gb., ISBN 3-8258-3162-0

Arie Goral-Sternheim
Jeckepotz
Eine jüdisch-deutsche Jugend 1914–1933.
Mit einem Vorwort von Jan Philipp
Reemtsma
Bd. 10, 1996, 208 S., 19,80 DM, br., ISBN 3-8258-3168-x

Suska Döpp
**Jüdische Jugendbewegung in Köln
1906–1938**
Von der Gründung des Gabriel-Riesser-Vereins im
Jahr 1906 bis zum endgültigen Verbot der jüdischen Jugendbünde in Deutschland im Jahr 1938
gab es in Köln eine zahlenmäßig starke und vitale
jüdische Jugendbewegung. Sie wurde schnell zu
einem vielfältigen und eigenwertigen Teil des jüdischen Lebens in Köln und umfaßte das gesamte
ideologisch-weltanschauliche Spektrum der jüdischen Jugendbewegung in Deutschland.
Über das Anliegen, einen Beitrag zur Wiederge-
winnung einer verlorengegangenen Überlieferung
im Bereich der Lokalgeschichte zu leisten, weist
dieser Band jedoch über den örtlichen Rahmen
hinaus. Hier wird am Beispiel einer Großge-
meinde ein Bild des bündischen Lebens auf der
untersten Organisationsebene der Jugendbewegung
nachgezeichnet. Im Mittelpunkt steht dabei neben
einer Darstellung der einzelnen Bünde in ihrer
weltanschaulich-ideologischen Ausprägung vor
allem das Verhältnis der Jugendorganisationen un-
tereinander, die Einbindung der Jugendbewegung
in die jüdische Gemeinschaft Kölns sowie in die
allgemeine städtische Jugendpflege.
Bd. 11, 1998, 256 S., 39,80 DM, br., ISBN 3-8258-3210-4

Martin Sieg
Im Schatten der Wolfschanze
Hitlerjunge auf der Suche nach Sinn. Autobiographische Skizze eines Zeitzeugen
Ein Zeitzeuge, Jahrgang 1927, der in der Nähe
des Führerhauptquartiers "Wolfschanze" groß
geworden ist, berichtet über seine ihn herausfor-
dernden Erlebnisse während der Hitlerzeit und
des Krieges. Die gezielte Beeinflussung durch
die NS-Ideologen, die Erschütterungen während
der Kampfhandlungen und die Erlebnisse von
Sinnlosigkeit nach dieser Zeit haben bei dem
damals noch Jugendlichen prägende Spuren und
eine geistige Unruhe hinterlassen. Besonders die
unfaßbaren Verbrechen des Holocaust lösten bei
seiner Flakhelfer-Generation die beunruhigenden
Fragen aus: "Wird jeder so, wenn man ihn läßt?
Könnte man selbst so werden? Gibt es dagegen
keinen Schutz?" (Zuckmayer). Angesichts der
schrecklichen Ereignisse gilt es, der Wahrheit über
den rätselhaften Menschen so objektiv wie möglich auf die Spur zu kommen. Der Autor fragt:
*Wird der aggressiv fanatische Haß des "Kain im
Menschen" weiterhin tödliche Folgen haben, so
daß die unmenschlichen Grausamkeiten von ge-
stern sich wiederholen können?*
*Kann die Menschheit einen Schutz gegen sich
selbst errichten und den Haß überwinden?*
*Kommt der verunsichert suchende Mensch der
aufklärenden Wahrheit näher, wenn er DEN be-
fragt, der hinter den Geheimnissen des von ihm
geschaffenen Lebens steht?*
*Ist der "neue Mensch", den Christus verkörpert,
ein Wegweiser aus der Sackgasse heraus, durch
den verläßlicher Lebenssinn in den Blick kommt?*
Bd. 12, 1997, 216 S., 29,80 DM, br., ISBN 3-8258-3288-0

LIT Verlag Münster – Hamburg – London
Bestellungen über:
Grevener Str. 179 48159 Münster
Tel.: 0251 – 23 50 91 – Fax: 0251 – 23 19 72
e-Mail: lit@lit-verlag.de – http://www.lit-verlag.de
Preise: unv. PE

Arie Goral-Sternheim; Walter Lovis
Um Mitternacht
1. Auflage – Jerusalem 1944
Bd. 13, Herbst 2000, 88 S., 19,80 DM, br,
ISBN 3-8258-3892-7

Hermann Görgen
Ein Leben gegen Hitler
Geschichte und Rettung der "Gruppe Görgen". Autobiographische Skizzen. Mit Geleitworten von I. Bubis, O. Lafontaine und M. Abelein

Frederic Forsyth, von Hause aus Journalist, stellt sich in seinem Roman "Icon" ("Das schwarze Manifest") die Frage: Ist es möglich, daß in Rußland ein charismatischer Führer – wie seinerzeit Hitler in Deutschland – an die Macht gelangt? Wiederholt sich also die Geschichte?

Doch verlassen wir die Gegenwart und gehen in die zwanziger Jahre, in denen unsere Handlung beginnt.

Hermann Görgen schildert seine Geschichte, er mußte erleben, wie Hitler gewählt wurde. Das ist allgemein bekannt; weniger bekannt ist, daß das Saarland damals nicht zum Deutschen Reich gehörte, sondern durch den Völkerbund verwaltet wurde. 1935 wählen die Saarländer den Anschluß an das Deutsche Reich. Görgen flieht, doch auch seine neue Heimat Österreich erliegt 1938 dem "Heim ins Reich-Gedanken".

Görgen muß erneut fliehen - diesmal in die Tschechoslowakei. Der Staat zerfällt und die Westmächte halten still. Sie halten genauso still wie Frederic Forsyth es in seinem Roman in Bezug auf die russische Entwicklung beschreibt. Hermann Görgen flieht in die Schweiz, doch auch sie bietet als neutraler Staat nicht jedem Flüchtling dauerhaften Schutz.

Politisch scheiterte Görgen, erfolgreich war er mit seiner "Gruppe Görgen", für die Rettung von achtundvierzig Flüchtlingen nach Brasilien zu verdanken ist.

In der Nachkriegszeit ins Saarland zurückgekehrt, setzt sich Görgen als Mitglied der "Christlichen Volkspartei des Saarlandes" und als Generaldirektor des "Saarländischen Rundfunks" für ein europäisches Saarland ein, mußte aber den Beginn einer Entwicklung in Richtung eines Anschlusses an die junge Bundesrepublik Deutschland erleben. Eine zukunftsweisende politische Vorstellung – gedacht einige Jahrzehnte zu früh.

Hermann Görgen war ein Föderalist, dessen Ideen insbesondere für das heutige Osteuropa mit seinen nationalen Konflikten Geltung besitzen.

Ein Buch über ihn und sein Leben kann nur ein Buch aktiven Erinnerns sein. Die Geschichte kann sich wiederholen, es kommt auf uns alle an, dies zu verhindern.

Hermann Görgen, 1908 in Wallerfangen/Saar geboren, promovierte an der Universität Bonn über den Philosophen und Pädagogen Friedrich Wilhelm Foerster. Als katholischer Oppositioneller arbeitete er 1934 bei der von Johannes Hoffmann gegründeten "Neuen Saarpost", ehe ihn seine Flucht an diverse inner- und außereuropäische Standorte verschlug.

Als Abgeordneter der CDU gehörte Hermann Görgen dem Deutschen Bundestag von 1957 bis 1961 an. Bis 1973 war er Beauftragter des Presse- und Informationsamtes der Bundesregierung für Sonderaufgaben in Lateinamerika. Von 1960 bis zu seinem Tode 1994 leitete er die "Deutsch-Brasilianische Gesellschaft" und das Lateinamerikazentrum.

Für die Rettung der jüdischen Flüchtlinge in seiner "Gruppe Görgen" wurde er 1993 vom Holocaust Memorial Center in Detroit mit dem "Righteousness Award", dem Holocaust-Gerechtigkeitsorden, ausgezeichnet.

Bd. 15, 1997, 256 S., 34,80 DM, br., ISBN 3-8258-3457-3

Barbara Rohr
Verwurzelt im Ortlosen
Einblicke in Leben und Werk von Simone Weil

Dieses Buch vermittelt Einblicke in Leben, Persönlichkeit und Werk einer ungewöhnlichen und vieldeutigen Frau. Wie lebte eine Frau, die in einer Epoche äußerer und innerer Umbrüche und großer Katastrophen vieles war, was unvereinbar scheint: Philosophieprofessorin und Sozialrevolutionärin, Intellektuelle und Gewerkschafterin, engagierte Pädagogin und politische Publizistin, Fabrikarbeiterin, Winzerin und Autorin religiöser Texte, Pazifistin und Soldatin, geistig hochbefähigt aber gesellschaftlich erfolglos, Jüdin, die zum Judentum keine Beziehung fand, Emigrantin und Widerstandskämpferin, Kirchenkritikerin und Mystikerin...? Wie lebte eine Frau, die sich den gesellschaftlich angebotenen Modellen der Frauenrolle verweigerte, die sich dem Status-Quo-Denken entzog, die Tätigkeiten und Berufe wechselte, die mit ihrem Leben experimentierte, die sich widerständisch-kämpferisch und ergeben zugleich nicht in politische und religiöse Glaubenssysteme einbinden ließ und sich stets dem Anderen, dem Unbekannten, Neuen und Fremden öffnete? Wie lebte und starb eine Frau, deren Leben trotz aller spirituellen Kraft mit 34 Jahren endete und die davon überzeugt war, für die Nachwelt eine Botschaft hinterlassen zu können? Dieser Botschaft, die Simone Weil gelebt hat, versucht die Autorin nachzugehen und auf deren Aktualität hinzuweisen.

Bd. 16, 2000, 160 S., 39,80 DM, br., ISBN 3-82582-4658-x

LIT Verlag Münster – Hamburg – London

Bestellungen über:
Grevener Str. 179 48159 Münster
Tel.: 0251 – 23 50 91 – Fax: 0251 – 23 19 72
e-Mail: lit@lit-verlag.de – http://www.lit-verlag.de

Preise: unv. PE